Translation and Own-language Activities

Cambridge Handbooks for Language Teachers

This series, now with 50 titles, offers practical ideas, techniques and activities for the teaching of English and other languages providing inspiration for both teachers and trainers.

Recent titles in this series:

Translation and Own-language Activities

Philip Kerr

Consultant and editor: Scott Thornbury

CAMBRIDGE
UNIVERSITY PRESS

CAMBRIDGE
UNIVERSITY PRESS

University Printing House, Cambridge CB2 8BS, United Kingdom

Cambridge University Press is part of the University of Cambridge.

It furthers the University's mission by disseminating knowledge in the pursuit of
education, learning and research at the highest international levels of excellence.

www.cambridge.org
Information on this title: www.cambridge.org/9781107645783

© Cambridge University Press 2014

First published 2014

Printed in Italy by Rotolito Lombarda S.p.A.

A catalogue record for this publication is available from the British Library

Library of Congress Cataloguing in Publication data
Kerr, Philip, 1959-
Translation and own-language activities / Philip Kerr.
    pages cm. -- (Cambridge handbooks for language teachers)
Includes index.
ISBN 978-1-107-64578-3 (pbk.)
1. English language--Study and teaching--Foreign speakers. 2. Second
language acquisition. 3. Translating and interpreting--Study and teaching.

I. Title.

 PE1128.A2K417 2014

 428.2'4--dc23

                                                        2013040424

ISBN 978-1-107-64578-3 Paperback

Contents

Thanks

My first thanks go to Helen Forrest, Scott Thornbury, Jo Garbutt and Karen Momber for all their work in the commissioning and editing of this book. Thanks, too, to the anonymous reviewers. I would also like to thank Cambridge University Press for continuing to publish books for teachers of this kind.

For their willingness to share their ideas, for their readiness to try out my ideas, and for their help with other languages, I owe a debt of gratitude to Mark Andrews, Iskra Anguelova, Ellie Boyadzhieva, Lindsay Clandfield, Hugh Dellar, Ben Goldstein, Syana Harizanova, Nicky Hockly, Roger Hunt, Ceri Jones, Andrea Kerr, Ella Kerr, Tamas Lorincz, Roger Marshall, Anna-Elisabeth Mayer, Melania Paduraru, Nina Tsvetkova, and George Woollard.

Acknowledgements

Text

The authors and publishers acknowledge the following sources of copyright material and are grateful for the permissions granted. While every effort has been made, it has not always been possible to identify the sources of all the material used, or to trace all copyright holders. If any omissions are brought to our notice, we will be happy to include the appropriate acknowledgements on reprinting.

Cambridge University Press for the texts on pp. 53 and 55 from *The New Cambridge English Course 2 Student's book* by Michael Swan and Catherine Walter, 1990. Copyright © Cambridge University Press 1990. Reproduced with permission;

Cambridge University Press for the texts on p. 61 from *Diccionario Cambridge Klett Mini English-Spanish*, 2004. Copyright © Ernst KLETT Sprachen GmbH, Stuttgart and Cambridge University Press 2004. Reproduced with permission;

Cambridge University Press for the texts on pp. 61 and 135 from *Diccionario Bilingue Cambridge Compact, Spanish-English*, 2009. Copyright © Cambridge University Press 2009. Reproduced with permission;

Screenshots on p. 66 used with permission from Microsoft;

Text on p. 79 from *Pride and Prejudice* by Jane Austen, published by T. Egerton, Whitehall, 1813;

Text on p. 82 adapted from *The Hitchhiker's Guide to the Galaxy* by Douglas Adams, published by Pan Books, 1979;

Google for the text on p. 88 from 'Find out how our translations are created', *Google Translate*, http://translate.google.co.uk/about/. Google and the Google logo are registered trademarks of Google Inc. Used with permission;

Text 'To Inform One'self of a Person' on p. 91 from *English as she is Spoke* by Pedro Carolino, published by Appleton & Co., 1883;

Cambridge University Press for the texts on pp. 97, 145–146 from *face2face Pre-intermediate Student's Book with DVD-ROM Second edition* by Chris Redston and Gillie Cunningham, 2012. Copyright © Cambridge University Press 2012. Reproduced with permission;

Wordle for the Word clouds on p. 99 www.wordle.net. Reproduced with permission;

Cambridge University Press for the text on p. 105 from *What's It Like? Student's book* by Joanne Collie and Alex Martin, 2000. Copyright © Cambridge University Press 2000. Reproduced with permission;

Cambridge University Press for the text on pp. 107–108 from *Interchange Student's Book Level 2 Third edition* by Jack C. Richards, Jonathan Hull and Susan Proctor, 2005. Copyright © Cambridge University Press 2005. Reproduced with permission;

Cambridge University Press for the texts on pp. 111 and 115 from *English Unlimited Coursebook with e-Portfolio Pre-intermediate* by Alex Tilbury, Theresa Clementson, Leslie Anne Hendra and David Rea, 2010. Copyright © Cambridge University Press 2010. Reproduced with permission;

Curtis Brown Group Ltd for the poem 'Like a Beacon' on p. 119 from *The Fat Black Woman's Poems* by Grace Nichols, published by Virago, 1984. Reproduced with permission of Curtis Brown Group Ltd, London on behalf of Grace Nichols. Copyright © Grace Nichols 1984;

British National Corpus for the text on p. 135. Data cited herein have been extracted from the British National Corpus Online service, managed by Oxford University Computing Services on behalf of the BNC Consortium. All rights in the texts cited are reserved.

Photos

The authors and publishers acknowledge the following sources of copyright material and are grateful for the permissions granted. While every effort has been made, it has not always been possible to identify the sources of all the material used, or to trace all copyright holders. If any omissions are brought to our notice, we will be happy to include the appropriate acknowledgements on reprinting.

p. 3 © Bettmann/CORBIS; p. 8 © Lebrecht Music & Arts/Corbis; p 46 From Redston, C. (2006) *face2face* Starter Student's Book, Cambridge: Cambridge University Press, p. 6; p. 75 'The Scholemaster' by Roger Ascham, published in London in 1571 (engraving), English School, (16th century) (after) / Private Collection / The Bridgeman Art Library; p. 90 (left) © Aurora Photos / Alamy; p. 90 (right) © Bon Appetit / Alamy; p. 99 Word clouds (Wordle) on the plot of *Lost in Translation* (2003); p.111 Tilbury, A., Clementson, T., Hendra, L. & Rea, D. (2010) English Unlimited B1, Cambridge: Cambridge University Press, p. 99; p. 137 (all three photos) ©Philip Kerr; p. 147 photo ©Philip Kerr.

Acknowledgements

1   Introduction

Why this book?

How to deal with mother tongue in an English class??

▶ No matter what nationality you are Mother tongue is always there interfering in our lessons.

▶ [Translating in the classroom] got so out of hand, that even I was looking up Spanish and (heaven forbid) writing translations on the board. After a few months of this, I realized that this has to stop and stop NOW.

▶ I work at a university prep school where using the mother tongue is forbidden but most of us use our mother tongue time to time as we feel the necessity of it.

▶ We treat the mother tongue as a problem because of the stupidity of our immersion methodology.

Figure 1.1: Blog postings at eltcommunity.com (2009–2010)

The use of the learner's own language in language teaching is a contentious issue. It is a topic that has been largely ignored in the most widely used teacher training manuals for English language teachers and on UK-based pre- and in-service training courses such as CELTA. (Early editions of some handbooks (Scrivener, 1994; Harmer, 1983) paid very little attention to the use of the students' own language in language classrooms. Both writers, however, have more recently made clear that they consider this an important issue.) It is also a topic which has featured very infrequently at ELT conferences in the last twenty-five years. Many language teaching organisations (from schools and school chains to language departments in colleges and universities) have policies banning the use of the mother tongue in language teaching classes.

There has been a steady stream of dissent (e.g. Bolitho, 1983; Atkinson, 1987; Prodromou, 2002), but, it seems, these voices have not been widely heard. At the same time, many teachers have continued to use the language that they share with their students. Research (Copland & Neokleous, 2011) tells us that many of these teachers under-report the amount of L1 they use in the class, suggesting that they do so with a sense of guilt. Luke Prodromou (2002, p. 5) has suggested that this guilt has cramped the potential of translation as a classroom resource.

Language teachers who use their mother tongue in the classroom, even teachers who write translations on the board, should be reassured. 2010 saw the publication of Guy Cook's award-winning *Translation in Language Teaching*. Critical reaction to the book has revealed an academic consensus on the role and use of the mother tongue. Such respected names as Vygotsky, Halliday and Widdowson were already on record as advocates of own-language use in learning another language.

Following publication of Cook's book, a string of well-known ELT trainers, writers and researchers (e.g. Jane Willis, Tessa Woodward and Rod Bolitho) supported the use of L1 when interviewed by the British Council for a series of YouTube videos (British Council, 2010). New editions of the teacher training manuals have begun to include sections on mother-tongue use in language teaching. The pendulum has swung so far that some researchers and practitioners are claiming that strictly monolingual learning environments may actually be detrimental to language learning. Perhaps the most forceful promotion of the use of the students' own language was put forward by Butzkamm & Caldwell (2009).

Whilst there is no shortage of evidence that principled use of L1 in the foreign language class can be beneficial, there is a shortage of practical material for language teachers. This book is intended to fill that gap.

Recent years have seen rapid advances in machine translation and the growing availability of free software such as good online bilingual dictionaries, online translation tools, and smartphone apps. These improving technological tools have become available to both teachers and students, and their quality and popularity will improve further. Some of the practical ideas in this book will draw on such easy-to-use web tools (see Chapter 4).

The first page of this book has referred to 'mother tongue', 'L1' (first language) and the learner's 'own language'. Another term that might have been used is 'native language'. Throughout this book, my preferred term will be 'own language'. 'Mother tongue' is problematic since the language in question may not be that of the learner's mother. 'Native language' is unsatisfactorily vague. 'L1', which for a long time has been the most commonly used term, is potentially misleading, especially in today's multicultural and multilingual classrooms where the learner's 'L1' may actually be a second or third language. The term 'own language' was advocated by Cook (2010), and can refer to the learner's own language or the shared language of the classroom, other than English, when this is not the same. See *Multilingual contexts* on page 10.

Translation and translating

This book suggests a wide variety of activities that involve the learner's own language in some way. These range from using bilingual dictionaries to translating long texts. The point of all of them is to promote language learning, rather than to develop translation skills (although some teachers of Translation Studies will find new ideas here). The majority involve spoken interaction, rather than written translation. The kind of translation mostly associated with Translation Studies – literary translation – is unlikely to be of much value to the vast majority of language teachers, whose students are not yet at the level of C1 or C2 where they may begin to tackle sophisticated literary texts.

The activities are typically focused on the process of translating, as opposed to the end result. More often than not, there are no wrong or right answers. What counts are the learning opportunities that are presented along the way.

Traditional reasons against using the learner's own language

Criticism of translation as a learning/teaching tool goes back at least to Maximilian Delphinus Berlitz at the beginning of the twentieth century. Berlitz had two fundamental principles: (1) 'direct association of thought with the foreign speech and sound', and (2) 'constant and exclusive use of

Figure 1.2: Maximilian Delphinus
Berlitz

the foreign language'. These principles certainly led to commercial success, but his arguments have resonated more with the general public than with language specialists.

Berlitz advanced three main reasons for abandoning translation:

- Too much time is taken up using the learner's own language, and not enough in using the language to be learned.
- You never really get used to the 'spirit' of a foreign language if you study with translation. 'The learner has a tendency to base all he [sic] says upon what he would say in his mother tongue.' (Berlitz, 1916, pp. 3–4)
- 'A knowledge of a foreign tongue, acquired by means of translation, is necessarily defective and incomplete; for there is by no means for every word of one language, the exact equivalent in the other.' (Berlitz, 1916, p. 4)

Berlitz's first point will strike a chord with many people who have studied a language in very traditional settings, where, especially at lower levels, virtually all exchanges are in the students' own language. These exchanges typically consist mainly of explanations of grammar. It is clear to most people that extensive use of the target language in the classroom is preferable, but it does not follow that *all* classroom exchanges should be in this language. The fact that some teachers overuse the students' own language in translation-aided teaching cannot justify the complete exclusion of this language, especially if judicious use of it may generate large amounts of the target language.

Regarding Berlitz's second point, it is difficult to define exactly what the 'spirit' of a foreign language is. Berlitz may have been referring to the popular idea that, in order to use a language well, one must also learn to think like someone who has that language as their mother tongue. The idea is seductive, but it is also vague because it makes an enormous generalisation about the mindsets of people who share a language. As an idea, it may also not be very relevant in the twenty-first century where English is mostly used as a tool of global communication. In contexts where English is being learned to communicate with others from non-English speaking backgrounds, the 'spirit' of the language (if some sort of national culture is meant by this word) is neither here nor there.

Leaving aside the relationship between a language and a particular culture, there is a further difficulty with the idea of learning to think in another language. This idea is widespread and often reported by people who have achieved a high level of proficiency in another language. If successful language learners experience a 'eureka moment' when they begin to think in the other language, it seems reasonable to do everything possible in the classroom to bring that moment forward. One proponent of the Direct Method, E. V. Gatenby, wrote that our aim must be 'to get our pupils [...] to the stage where they can use English without having to think' (Gatenby, 1967, p. 70). He did not mean, of course, that the students should not think at all, but that they should learn 'to dissociate the two languages'. It is this pervasive belief that students need to separate the two languages that is usually at the heart of the exclusion of their own language from foreign language classrooms.

Whilst this attempt to separate the two languages may work well for some learners in some contexts, it is unlikely to work for all. There are two reasons for this. The first is that the human brain is not neatly compartmentalised into regions, with one language stored in one part of the brain, and another language in another part. Studies, such as research into word associations (e.g. Spivey & Hirsch, 2003), show clearly that the brain processes knowledge of two or more languages in parallel, at least to some extent. Languages cannot be separated out, even if we would like them to be. The second reason is that the vast majority of language learners do not need, and may not even wish, to achieve a level of proficiency which would permit 'thinking' in that language. The language of thought, it has been suggested (Turnbull & Dailey-O'Cain, 2009, p. 5), is inevitably the students' first language, except for those who have reached advanced levels (C1+). In other words, an English-only policy, however well-intentioned, may be both unrealistic and inappropriate to the majority of students.

Berlitz's third point – that there is no such thing as full word-for-word equivalences between language and that therefore a translation approach, which seems to promote a search for equivalences, will lead to a 'defective' and incomplete knowledge of the language – is superficially attractive, but does not stand up to scrutiny. Competence in any language, one's own or another, is necessarily an emergent phenomenon, whether it has been acquired by translation or not. We would not choose to use words like 'defective' these days: learners need to acquire a foreign language up to the level they need. An inability to appreciate the finer points of, say, poetry may not be terribly important.

The published critics of classroom translation, including Berlitz, have tended to paint worst-case scenarios of the dullest, driest, most relentless grammar-translation slog, held these up for ridicule (what one writer has called the 'And-now-who-will-take-the-next-sentence?' approach), and then used them as justification for rejecting all cross-lingual work. This logical fallacy does, however, lend support to the strongest, and possibly the only, reason for avoiding the use of the learner's own language in the foreign language classroom: the commercial imperative.

Many private schools sell themselves on their native-speaker teachers (who may not know the language of their students and who may be assumed to use something resembling a Direct Method approach). University departments sometimes pride themselves on their target-language-only policy, and these departments are often competing for the same students as the language schools. 'Native speaker is best' remains a commonly held folk belief in many, perhaps most, parts of the world, and so there is, and is likely to remain, a market for target-language-only teaching. We would be unwise to underestimate the significance in the classroom of the students' beliefs about the most effective language teaching methodology for them, even if these beliefs are not informed by the insights of applied linguistics.

The role of the learner's own language

It is beyond the ability of anyone to banish totally the learners' own language from a foreign language learning experience. Learning is, by definition, built upon previous learning, and the most significant resource that learners can bring to the language learning task is their existing linguistic knowledge – a substantial portion of which consists of knowledge about their own language. Learning is scaffolded, and, especially in the early stages of learning another language, it will be scaffolded, in part, on the language(s) they already know.

Whilst teachers can, perhaps, control the language their students speak, they cannot force them to think in the target language. Furthermore, the use of some translation techniques is one of the preferred learning strategies of most learners in most places (Atkinson, 1987). Like it or not, translating won't go away. It makes more sense for a teacher to use translation in a principled, overt way than to pretend that the students are not using it covertly.

There are a number of very powerful reasons (see below) why the use of the students' own language in the language classroom should not only be tolerated, but, at times, actively encouraged.

1   Own language as a point of reference

Evidence from both cognitive linguistics and neuroscience point strongly towards a role for the students' own language in the language classroom. In fact, Widdowson (2003) and others have argued that the neglect of translation has little to do with pedagogical principles or scientific research. New knowledge is constructed on a base of old knowledge. As long ago as 1934, Vygotsky wrote that learning a new language necessarily involves the use of one's own language 'as a mediator between the world of objects and the new language' (Vygotsky ed. Kozulin, 1986, p. 161). Neuroscience confirms that the initial acquisition of new words in a foreign language depends on the association of these items with corresponding own-language items in the learner's memory (Sousa, 2011, pp. 24–7).

It is commonly believed that the use of translation activities in the classroom can lead to 'negative transfer', where the learner falsely assumes an equivalence between corresponding forms in two languages (e.g. false friends). In the case of English and any other language, there are likely to be many more true 'friends' than false ones ('friendships' that can be efficiently explored through translation – see Activity 7.1). In the case of all languages, it is probably the case that the best and most efficient way to deal with 'negative transfer' is to compare the two languages directly.

A direct contrast between English and the learner's own language may also pay dividends in the study of grammar. Some aspects of the grammar of one's own language (e.g. word order) can be very hard to shake off when learning another language. Conscious awareness of what these are can help learners make progress in these areas. Translation is likely to be the most unambiguous and efficient way of achieving this awareness. See the introduction to Chapter 7 on page 121 for further discussion of contrastive analysis and for activities which directly juxtapose elements of English and the learner's own language.

2   The discourse of English language teaching

Disapproval of the use of the students' own language in the language classroom can be traced back historically. It is well documented (see *A brief history of own-language use in language teaching*, page 8). The world of English language teaching, or rather the world of ELT authors, conferences, books and journals, publishers and well-known lecturers, is dominated by a group of native speakers with close connections to English-speaking countries. In those English-speaking countries, most English classes are multicultural and multilingual, and translation is not an obvious option for the teacher (but see *Multilingual contexts*, page 10).

The discourse of ELT has been largely shaped by what Holliday (1994) would call BANA (British, Australasian and North American) people. Their interests have been informed by their experience of multilingual teaching contexts and translation has been off the radar. However, the reign of the native speaker is perhaps beginning to crumble. No longer custodians of the language, since the rise of English as a Lingua Franca (or English as an International Language), native speakers no longer hold a monopoly on influential posts in academia, publishing and professional organisations such as IATEFL.

With a growing voice in ELT discourse, non-native (or ELF) speaker teachers inevitably draw on their own experiences as language learners: predominantly monolingual and monocultural, and probably involving translation. Some may well disapprove of translation, but the issue of whether or not to allow the students' own language in the classroom remains high on the agenda.

3 *Intercultural competence*

It can be easy to forget the obvious. The point of language learning is, at least in part, to be able to communicate with and understand people from another culture. We might reasonably hope that intercultural understanding will lead to intercultural harmony (although this is not necessarily the case!). Culture, cultural identity and linguistic identity are closely linked. If a user of a language closely equates their identity with that language, the classroom banning of that language may cause tension. Especially at the start of the intercultural journey, outlawing the mother tongue seems almost wilfully misguided. Teachers presumably want to validate their students' linguistic and cultural identity, rather than suppress it.

The exploration and understanding of differences and similarities between cultures cannot avoid comparisons between at least two languages, and this means that translation cannot be avoided. Why on earth would any teacher *not* directly compare the most obvious linguistic manifestations of cultural difference (e.g. ways of saying *Hello*)? As a low-level learner of German, for example, I want to know exactly what *Grüss Gott* means and who it is used by, and the only way I can do that

---

Dragomans were translators, interpreters and go-betweens in the Ottoman Empire. Mostly Greeks, some rose to positions of great power and their world is marvelously evoked in the novels of Ismail Kadare. The role of dragomans was essentially one of mediating between cultures through different languages. The complexity of this mediation task is illustrated in the following example, in English, of the sort of thing a dragoman might have said, in Ottoman, to a sultan on behalf of an ambassador.

Having bowed my head in submission and rubbed my slavish brow in utter humility and complete abjection and supplication to the beneficent dust beneath the feet of my mighty, gracious, condescending, compassionate, merciful benefactor, my most generous and open-handed master, I pray that the peerless and almighty provider of remedies etc. etc.

It's fun to speculate what the original words of the ambassador to the dragoman might have been.

Figure 1.3: From Lewis, B. (2005) *From Babel to Dragomans: Interpreting the Middle East,* Oxford University Press USA, p. 26

is if someone explains it to me in another language that I already speak or read. The potential of translation for developing intercultural skills is high because it is the mediation of communication between two cultures. This skill of mediation has been identified in the Common European Framework of Reference for Languages (Council of Europe, 2001) as being on a par with language reception, language production and language interaction. It is perverse to promote mediation while banning the students' own language.

4   *Personal meanings, affect and anxiety*

It is generally accepted that it is a good thing for language learners to express personal meanings when they are practising the target language. At lower levels, especially, it is very difficult for learners to express their personal meanings (beyond answering simple questions such as *Do you like apples?*) without the linguistic resources to do so. If we want to help learners to express those personal meanings, it is a good idea to find out, in their own language, what it is they want to say. Banning the mother tongue would be counter-productive, to say the least.

It is also generally accepted that teachers should take some account of learners' preferred learning strategies. We know that most learners do prefer to use some elements of translation in their studies. Discovering that one of your preferred learning strategies is banned is unlikely to do much for your confidence. If this damages your belief in your possibility of success as a language learner, the less likely you are to succeed. Even occasional use of the learner's own language in some language learning contexts can help to reduce anxiety (particularly at lower levels) and promote hope.

5   *New technologies*

The existence of online translation tools is reason alone for language teachers to deal directly with translation issues in the classroom. Students are using and will use these tools for parts of their work, sometimes substantial parts, and so teachers need to be familiar with them. Issues arising from the use of online translation tools are explored further in Chapter 4. Students are often, of course, technologically more knowledgeable than their teachers, but they don't always know how to make best use of the technological skills they possess. We should consider helping our students to understand online translation tools in the same way that we would consider helping them to use a good monolingual dictionary or grammar book.

It is quite possible that good monolingual dictionaries will soon become a thing of the past. With the inexorable shift of dictionaries from hefty tomes to digitalised files and apps for smartphones, storage space has suddenly increased. Good monolingual dictionaries can now contain bilingual information, and some of the best dictionaries currently available are, in fact, bilingual dictionaries. Language learners need to know about resources such as these, as well as sites that offer free language learning programmes, such as duolingo.com and byki.com.

For younger and older learners, there are apps for fun bilingual word cards. For teachers and other authorities, there are programs to detect the use of online translation and plagiarism. For everyone, Web 2.0 tools provide possibilities for a greater variety of classroom activities and interactions involving two languages, and a number of the activities in this book use such tools. Translation, in short, is part of our technological future.

6 *Practicalities*

As almost every language teacher knows, the ability to quickly translate something can save a lot of time. If you were learning Pirahã, for example, you'd probably want your teacher, very early on, to explain in your own language that the word *xahoasai* can refer to green things, blue things, young children and unripe fruit (Everett, 2012). You would want someone to explain that there is a difference between hum speech, yell speech and normal speech, because speech which is hummed or yelled conveys different social meanings to that which is spoken in a normal tone. It would be quicker for everyone if they did this in your own language, rather than limiting their explanation to Pirahã, normal, hummed or yelled.

Translation is likely to be more time-efficient than demonstration, explanation or guided discovery approaches. It is also likely to be clearer. This is true of work with grammar, discourse, vocabulary and pronunciation.

Time is of the essence in all language teaching situations. Some corners will need to be cut. At the same time, most teachers will want to motivate their students and themselves, and one step is to inject variety into the class. The neglect of a wide choice of lively and communicative activities that involve translation would be rather wasteful.

A brief history of own-language use in language teaching

If you wanted to learn a language in 16th-century western Europe, one way of doing so was to go to a language school or get a private tutor. Among the most fashionable and influential educators of the time were the Valencian scholar Juan Luis Vives (1493–1540) and the English scholar, Roger Ascham (1515–1568). Vives and Ascham both recommended extensive use of reverse (or 'back') translation, an activity that involves translating a text from one language to another and then back again. Not everyone agreed with them. The Fleming Nicholas Cleynaerts (1495–1542) claimed that he taught his students in what could be described as a 16th-century precursor of the Direct Method: he used only Latin to teach Latin and claimed good results for his method. There is, however, ample testimony to the greater popularity of the approach of Vives and Ascham.

Figure 1.4: 16th century classroom

On the other side of the Mediterranean in Istanbul, the largest city of the western world at that time, there were schools for translators and interpreters, or 'dragomans' as they were known (see Figure 1.3, page 6). In newly conquered South America, the conquistadors and missionaries needed interpreters and these were trained. Learning a language and translating between two languages were inextricably linked activities.

From this time on, the steady growth in school provision across Europe (at least, for boys) was accompanied by the teaching of Latin and Greek, the Classical languages so beloved of Renaissance scholars. Known as 'grammar-translation', the standard classroom approach entailed translation of extracts from Classical authors, combined with writing exercises. When modern languages began to replace Latin and Greek in the curriculum in the 19th century, the teaching methodology remained largely unchanged. In some contexts even today, grammar-translation remains the norm. There were, however, some who questioned the appropriacy of this approach, and the beginning of the debate about the use of the learner's own language can be traced to this period.

The beginning of the 20th century saw a growing market for language schools, not least because of the development of rapid international transport. By the end of the century, these schools had grown into a multi-billion-dollar global business. By and large, they have tried to distinguish themselves from language teaching in state-run institutions, secondary and tertiary, where the use of the students' own language is much more common.

Precise figures are hard to come by because we rely on teachers reporting their own practices, but it would seem that the use of translation remains the norm in university teaching around the world. In secondary and primary schools, it is reasonable to assume that elements of translation or own-language use are unavoidable. There are, however, some important exceptions.

Own-language and other language policies

Educational language policies are not always informed by the most up-to-date research. The banning of the students' own language is one example of this, and in their review of current research, Hall & Cook (2012) indicate that there is now a substantial body of literature which supports own-language use.

Nevertheless, own-language use remains prohibited in many contexts. Around the globe, there are language schools that threaten to dismiss teachers who use translation in class. There are still schools that ask some teachers to pretend to be a different nationality. In universities which insist on English-only in English language classes, the policy is often driven by the fact that English is the medium of instruction for other academic courses. The inability of many students to cope with English as a medium of instruction is seen, in part, as the product of an over-reliance on the students' own language in primary and secondary schools. In an attempt to redress the balance, there has been a growth in university foundation courses, but, as some commentators (e.g. Mouhanna, 2009) have suggested, the problems in junior schooling may not be best solved by English-only instruction in universities.

If you are working in a context that is hostile to translation, you need to tread carefully. Collective attempts to change institutional policies are usually more effective than individual attempts, but even these may take time. For further discussion of attitudes towards own-language use in the language classroom, as well as a selection of activities which encourage students to reflect on their own attitudes, see Chapter 3.

Multilingual contexts

The main descriptions of the activities in this book assume that the teacher and the students speak the same language. In the overriding majority of teaching contexts, teachers and students do, indeed, share a language other than English. In such classrooms, teachers often report that their greatest problem is getting their students to *stop* using their own language and to start using English. I will suggest (especially in Chapter 6) that part (but only a part) of the solution to this problem is to allow, even to encourage, judicious use of the students' own language from time to time.

But what of the teacher who works in a multilingual environment (such as a language school in an English-speaking country)? Here, it is easier to motivate the students to speak English, but there may be ten or more different own-languages in one classroom, and, in the course of an academic year, many times more than that. Even if the teacher could speak all the students' languages, it is hard, or impossible, to imagine making any practical use of this extraordinary ability in the day-to-day business of teaching truly multilingual groups. The approach to teaching these classes is necessarily very different from the approach to teaching truly monolingual groups. Most obviously, the teacher will have to use only English. However, this does not mean that there is no place in these classrooms for the students' own languages.

Between the two kinds of class outlined above, there are many other possible own-language configurations. Here are just a few examples.

- A secondary school class in Catalonia where the majority of students speak Catalan at home, but some come from other language backgrounds (e.g. Spanish, Urdu, Romanian). These students use Catalan in the rest of their school classes. The teacher speaks Catalan and Spanish.
- A Volkshochschule (adult education institute) class in Vienna where the language background of the learners is very mixed (e.g. German, Turkish, Pashto, Urdu, Serbian). The teacher speaks German, but knowledge of the other languages is limited to what has been picked up in the course of teaching students from these language backgrounds.
- A language school class in Kiev where the language background of the learners is Ukrainian or Russian, but all can communicate in both languages. The teacher has only very elementary Ukrainian and Russian.
- A university class in Brussels where the majority of the students speak either Flemish or French at home. A minority speak other languages at home (e.g. Moroccan Arabic, Turkish, Greek), but all can speak French or Flemish, or both. The teacher's first language is Flemish, but she also speaks good French.

Even within one institution, there can be a number of different configurations. In a British language school, for example, there might be closed groups of teenagers in the school holidays, one-to-one classes, groups of executives studying business English or groups of teachers on language or methodology refresher courses.

In order to simplify a complex situation and to make some useful generalisations about the potential for own-language use in different classrooms, I have identified the following three basic types of class.

Type A

The teacher cannot use any language other than English in the classroom. The students do not have any shared language. However, they can and they will use their own language in the course of their

English language learning. They will probably use translation tools for their study, and they would benefit from guidance. They can also be encouraged to think about the differences between English and their own language, and to discuss the way that their English language use is informed by their own language background. This class is typically found in an English-speaking part of the world.

Type B

The teacher cannot use any language other than English in the classroom. The students have one or more shared languages, but they all share a community language (usually the language of their schooling). When there is more than one shared language, pair and group work are still possible because there is more than one student from each language group. The learning potential of comparison of one's own language with two or more other languages is rich and should be exploited.

Type C

The teacher can use the students' own language or a shared community language.

All of the activities in this book (except Activity 3.4: *Learn my language*) can be used with Type C classes. At the end of each activity, you will find a note indicating whether it can be used with Type A and Type B classes. The majority can be used in Type B classes, even though the teacher cannot speak the same language as the students. A surprisingly high number of activities can be used in Type A classes. In some of these, the possibility of collaboration between students is lost, but the activities remain valuable nevertheless.

The examples that I have provided are limited to a small number of European languages, but are applicable to others. This limitation has been dictated by my own experience (which has mostly been in western Europe) and by a desire to use only the Roman alphabet, so that all readers of this book can make some sense of what is being exemplified.

Translation and teacher education

If language teachers come across translation during their training as teachers, there is a good chance that it will be as part of their university language studies when they attend classes that tackle a literary text using a 'And-now-who-will-take-the-next-sentence?' methodology. It is unlikely that they will be asked to build reflective bridges between the language and pedagogical modules of their courses. It would be a good idea for language lecturers and translation lecturers to talk to each other more often.

For the (predominantly native-speaker) teacher trainees following courses like the Cambridge CELTA or DELTA, translation has been largely ignored and even frowned upon (although this depends on the centre running the course). There are signs, however, that this is changing.

The simple addition to training courses of a seminar or two devoted to translation and own-language use may not be especially fruitful. Developing teachers learn much more by example than anything else, so a training course that wants to encourage trainees to make the most of the opportunities that translation offers needs, in advance, to work out what its own approach to code-switching will be. Consideration will need to be given to the language of instruction, the language of administration, the language of feedback, and the contexts in which the teachers are likely to be working.

Seminars will, however, be necessary in order to explore the principles that will determine language policies in the classroom. Novice teachers need to understand when own-language use is appropriate, and, equally importantly, when it is not.

The activities in the appendix to this book are intended specifically for teacher development contexts; others can easily be adapted for them. Trainers will want to think about their own code-switching, and, from the start of a course, the issue of mother tongue use can be prominent.

Suggestions for using this book

Most 'recipe books' for teachers contain off-the-peg lessons, often with photocopiable materials, that can be used exactly as they are presented. This book is rather different. Here, the majority of activities are activity types, as opposed to individual activities that exploit a particular text or focus on a particular grammar point or lexical set. By the very nature of activities that involve two languages, described in a book for readers of many different language backgrounds, it is not possible to provide photocopiable material which will be appropriate to everyone. Many examples of materials are given, but these will need to be adapted to your own teaching context.

That is not to say, however, that teachers will need to spend inordinate amounts of time preparing lessons that include these activities. Many of them require no preparation at all; others require only minimal preparation.

For most readers, I imagine that the most important chapters will be Chapter 2 (*Techniques*) and Chapter 4 (*Tools*). These techniques and tools underpin many of the ideas suggested in the other chapters, and I would recommend reading these before exploring the other suggestions.

Some readers, including myself, prefer to work through a book page by page from the beginning to the end. With books of this kind, however, there is no strong reason not to flick through, looking for anything that takes one's fancy, or to jump around haphazardly. When compiling the activities, I tried as far as possible to make sure that activities are doable:

- with low level, high level and mixed level classes
- with both teenage and adult students
- with both small and large classes
- in contexts where teachers are using a coursebook and where they are not.

For the great majority of general English teachers, therefore, the great majority of the activities here will be practicable.

Suggestions for further reading

Anyone who is interested in the topic of translation should read David Bellos's best-selling and entertaining *Is that a Fish in your Ear?* (2011). A cultural history of translation, written for the general reader, it contains much that will fascinate and inspire language teachers.

For teachers who are interested in further exploring the reasons for and against using the students' own language in the language classroom, the first port of call should be Guy Cook's award-winning *Translation in Language Teaching* (2011). As a companion piece to Guy Cook's book, I would also strongly recommend an article that he co-wrote with Graham Hall, entitled 'Own-language use in language teaching and learning' (Hall & Cook, 2011). This provides a detailed survey of the academic literature on own-language use.

For practical classroom ideas, *Using the Mother Tongue* (Deller & Rinvolucri, 2002) contains many good ideas, some of which I have drawn on in this book. *Multiple voices in the translation classroom* (González Davies, 2004) is intended primarily for teachers of translation, but contains many excellent suggestions which will interest language teachers. Again, I have drawn on some of her ideas in this book. Finally, *Translation* (Duff, 1989) contains a number of ideas that will be of interest to teachers of higher-level students.

References

Atkinson, D. (1987) 'The mother tongue in the classroom: a neglected resource?', *ELT Journal* Vol 41/4, pp. 241–7. Available online at: http://eltj.oxfordjournals.org/content/41/4/241.full. pdf+html. [Last accessed 01 July 2013]

Bellos, D. (2011) *Is that a Fish in your Ear?*, London: Penguin.

Berlitz, M.D. (1916) *Method for Teaching Modern Languages, English Part, First Book*, New York: Berlitz.

Bolitho, R. (1983) 'Talking Shop: The communicative teaching of English in non-English-speaking countries', *ELT Journal* Vol 37/3, pp. 235–42. Available online by subscription at: http://eltj. oxfordjournals.org/content/37/3/235.full.pdf+html. [Last accessed 01 July 2013]

British Council (2010) *Teaching English: Interviews*. Available online at: http://www.youtube.com/ playlist?list=PLF43F295FE0263E59. [Last accessed 01 July 2013]

Butzkamm, W. & Caldwell, J.A.W. (2009) *The Bilingual Reform: a paradigm shift in foreign language teaching*, Tübingen: Narr Studienbücher.

Cook, G. (2010) *Translation in Language Teaching*, Oxford: Oxford University Press.

Copland, F. & Neokleous, G. (2011) 'L1 to teach L2: complexities and contradictions', *ELT Journal* Vol 65/3, pp. 270–80. Available online by subscription at: http://eltj.oxfordjournals. org/content/65/3/270.full. [Last accessed 01 July 2013]

Council of Europe (2001), *Common European Framework of Reference for Languages*. Available online at: http://www.coe.int/t/dg4/linguistic/source/framework_en.pdf. [Last accessed 01 July 2013]

Deller, S. & Rinvolucri, M. (2002) *Using the Mother Tongue*, Peaslake, Surrey: Delta.

Duff, A. (1989) *Translation*, Oxford: Oxford University Press.

Everett, D. (2012) *Language: The Cultural Tool*, London: Profile Books.

Gatenby, E.V. (1967) 'Translation in the classroom' in W. R. Lee (ed.) *ELT Selections 2: Articles from the Journal 'English Language Teaching'*, London: Oxford University Press, pp. 65–70.

González Davies, M. (2004) *Multiple voices in the translation classroom*, Amsterdam: John Benjamins.

Hall, G. & Cook, G. (2012) 'Own-language use in language teaching and learning' *Language Learning* 45.3, pp. 271–308. Available online at: http://journals.cambridge.org/action/displayAbst ract?fromPage=online&aid=8614395. [Last accessed 01 July 2013]

Harmer, J. (1983) *The Practice of English Language Teaching*, Harlow: Longman.

Holliday, A. (1994) *Appropriate Methodology and Social Context*, Cambridge: Cambridge University Press.

Lewis, B. (2005) *From Babel to Dragomans: Interpreting the Middle East*, Oxford: Oxford University Press.

Mouhanna, M. (2009) 'Re-examining the role of L1 in the EFL Classroom' *UGRU Journal*, Volume 8, Spring 2009, pp. 1–19. Available online at: www.ugr.uaeu.ac.ae/acads/ugrujournal/docs/REL1.pdf. [Last accessed 01 July 2013]

Prodromou, L. (2002) 'The role of the mother tongue in the classroom', *IATEFL Issues 166*.

Prodromou, L. (2002) Prologue to Deller, S. & Rinvolucri, M., *Using the Mother Tongue*, Peaslake, Surrey: Delta Publishing.

Scrivener, J. (1994) *Learning Teaching: A Guidebook for English Language Teachers*, Oxford: Macmillan.

Sousa, D. A. (2011) *How the ELL Brain Learns*, Thousand Oaks, CA: Corwin Books.

Spivey, M. V. & Hirsch, J. (2003) 'Shared and separate systems in bilingual language processing: Converging evidence from eyetracking and brain imaging', *Brain and Language*, 86, pp. 70–82.

Turnbull, M. & Dailey-O'Cain, J. (eds) (2009) *First Language Use in Second and Foreign Language Learning*, Bristol: Multilingual Matters.

Vygotsky, L. (1986) *Thought and Language*, newly revised and edited by Alex Kozulin, Cambridge, Mass.: MIT Press.

Widdowson, H. (2003) *Defining Issues in English Language Teaching*, Oxford: Oxford University Press.

Glossary

alignment   the process of identifying with or matching the thoughts or behaviour of someone else

back translation   translating from one language, and then back into the original language

bilingualism   the use of two languages by one speaker or group of speakers ('multilingualism' is the use of more than two languages): there are more bilingual or multilingual language users around the world than there are people who can speak only one language

bilingualised   a bilingualised dictionary combines explanations of words in L2 with translations in L1

code-switching   switching between two languages

cognate   a word in one language which has the same (or similar) form and origin as a word in another language

contrastive analysis   comparing two languages in order to see their similarities and differences with a view to improving competence in one of them

digital literacy   the ability to use digital technologies effectively and critically

Direct Method   an approach to language teaching which does not use the learner's own language; it focuses on spoken language, adopts a non-rule-based approach to grammar, and the language is practised through question-and-answer drills

false friend   a word or phrase in one language which looks or sounds like a word or phrase in another language, but which has a different meaning

grammar-translation   a traditional approach to language teaching where students are given grammatical rules and then practise them through translation exercises

interference   first language interference (or mother tongue interference) is the way in which knowledge of, or habits in, one's first language may lead to errors in another language; also referred to as language transfer or negative transfer

L1   the learner's first language (sometimes called 'mother tongue')

L2   the learner's second language – the language they are trying to learn – although this may, in fact, be a third or fourth language

language transfer   see 'interference'

learning style   the usual approach of individual learners (e.g. convergers, divergers, assimilators, accommodators) to learning situations

metalanguage   the language that is used to talk about language (e.g. grammatical terminology)

negative transfer   see 'interference'

recasting   reformulating something that a student has said in a more appropriate or more accurate way

reverse translation   translating from one language, and then back into the original language (back translation)

sandwiching   during teacher talk, when the teacher uses a word or a phrase that is unlikely to be known by the students, the insertion of a translation in the students' own language, and then the repetition of the unknown word or phrase

scaffolding   helping learners to carry out a particular learning task by, for example, clarifying/simplifying the task or giving them language support

target language   the language that the teacher is teaching and the learners are trying to learn

translanguaging   similar to code-switching, the process of mixing elements from two languages

2 Techniques

Techniques and activities

In the same way that learners can be said to have a dominant learning style, teachers have a dominant teaching style. This is informed by a set of beliefs and attitudes (which are often unexamined) and is manifested by the teacher's actions in the classroom. These actions include such things as the way we talk to students, the way that we manage a class and the basic teaching techniques that we use. Because these actions or behaviours are deeply rooted in our beliefs, we tend to repeat them, and the more we repeat them, the more automatic they become. They are hard to change.

A teacher's choice of materials or activities is, on the contrary, much more susceptible to change. Teacher-training workshops and teachers' handbooks (such as this one) generally concentrate on materials and activities. When we plan our lessons, we tend to think first and foremost about activities – those that we particularly like or that we know will 'work well' – and most of us are keen to add to our repertoire and experiment with new ideas. Most of the chapters in this book will provide suggestions for materials and activities, but this chapter, the first main chapter, focuses on the most basic routines of our teaching: techniques. It is with these that I recommend that you begin to experiment.

Own-language use: psychological reasons

In most classrooms, there is no problem getting students to speak their own language! The problem is more likely to be getting them to stop using their own language and start using English. An English-only policy, either in individual classrooms or in entire institutions, is a well-intentioned but sometimes misguided attempt to deal with this problem. However paradoxical it may seem, the occasional, principled use of the students' own language (by both the teacher and the students themselves) may lead to greater and richer use of English.

If we understand the reasons for our students' reluctance or refusal to speak English, we may be better prepared to deal with the problem. It is easy to attribute such reluctance to laziness or a simple lack of cooperation, but these are possibly proximate, rather than ultimate, causes. The lack of motivation may have deeper roots. These could lie in:

- the students feeling uncomfortable or embarrassed about attempting to communicate in a foreign language (which they do not feel very proficient with) to someone who speaks their own language
- the students' failure to understand the point of attempting to speak in English, knowing that their speech will probably contain errors
- the students' antipathy towards the English language, the learning context or the teacher
- the students' tiredness.

An English-only policy may exacerbate these underlying problems, rather than address them. Using the students' own language may, at times, be a more direct and more efficient way of dealing with these issues.

A number of studies have looked at the way that teachers use the students' own language in their English classes. Looking at interpersonal relations in the classroom, Lynne Cameron (2001, pp. 201–4) has suggested that we could divide these uses into two main groups:

- Alignment – by using the students' own language, teachers can, in some ways, align themselves with them, to show that they are 'on their side'. This may be, for example, to indicate that they understand their problems. In contrast, using the target language, English, may reinforce the perception of difference between teacher and students, since the teacher already has the competence in English which the students aspire to.
- Emphasis – switching from one language to another may give greater weight to what is being said. In a class where English is the primary means of instruction, changing to the students' own language may give added weight to what is being said. For this reason, teachers will often choose to use the students' own language when they need to discipline them.

Using the students' own language, therefore, can and will affect the interpersonal dynamic of a classroom.

Own-language use: other reasons

Both users and learners of other languages code-switch: they switch between languages. This can happen between turns in a conversation, when a speaker begins in one language, switches temporarily to the other language, before returning to the original language. It can even happen in the middle of a short utterance, when a couple of words in one language are embedded in the other language. It is a feature of both spoken and written language (it is very common, for example, on social media websites such as Facebook). This is a normal and natural part of being bilingual. In this light, it is hard to justify the complete banishing of code-switching in a language classroom.

There are many possible reasons for code-switching, but in an English language classroom these are likely to include, for both teachers and students, the following (in addition to the interpersonal reasons discussed above):

- Need: the user lacks the necessary vocabulary for what they want to express. They may also lack the language that is needed for paraphrasing.
- Appropriacy: some things may seem to be better said in one language than the other.
- Economy: it is quicker and easier to code-switch than to stick to one language.
- Clarity: code-switching may contribute to better understanding of an intended communication.

All of these reasons can be very powerful in themselves. In combination, they can be more powerful still. A number of the techniques which are described in this chapter involve elements of code-switching. It has been argued in recent years that the job of language teachers is to push their learners towards competent bilingualism, rather than to set them the unattainable (for most learners) goal of native-speaker-like competence. If this is true, code-switching is a skill to be practised and developed.

Incorporating techniques into your repertoire

The use of teaching techniques that involve the learners' own language can, therefore, be justified when they are a means to the end of promoting their learning of English. A word of caution is needed, however. If the techniques in this chapter (and the activities in the rest of this book) are overused, you will be restricting your students' exposure to English. It is important, as Jayne Moon reminds us, that we keep our main goal in mind, 'as you are likely to be [your students'] main source of English input' (Moon, 2000, p. 67).

But exactly when and how often should we use these techniques? Unfortunately, there are no simple answers. The first consideration, which will be no surprise to most teachers, is the level of proficiency of the learners. The lower the level, the more learners rely on their first language when attempting to make sense of or express themselves in a new language. Research suggests that low-level learners are most likely to transfer knowledge about vocabulary and pronunciation from their own language to the target language (Agustin Llach, 2009). At higher levels, learners have more information about the new language at their disposal and are consequently less dependent on their own language. It might seem that banning the learners' own language at lower levels of language learning is the best way to avoid an over-reliance on it, and this is one of the reasons that are often given for an English-only policy. However, no ban can prevent learners from transferring their existing language knowledge. It makes a lot more sense to guide our students in their transfer of language knowledge, than to leave them to their own devices or to pretend that such transfer is not taking place. Techniques that make explicit both the similarities and differences between English and learners' own language will be particularly beneficial at lower levels.

In the same way, younger learners will benefit from bilingual techniques. Younger learners, who are typically at a low level of proficiency anyway, seem to be less able than adults to judge which features of their own language can be transferred to English. Explicit help and guidance of a bilingual nature is likely to be of more use to them than a policy of English only.

At lower levels and at younger ages, therefore, we are likely to need bilingual techniques more than at higher levels with more mature learners. These are not, however, the only things that a teacher needs to bear in mind. As important will be the learning objectives of the particular activity during which the techniques are used. The teacher will also need to think about their students' previous language learning experiences and the interpersonal dynamics of the classroom at any given moment, as well as the broader curricular objectives and institutional context of the course of study. Decisions about exactly when and how often these techniques are used can only be taken on the spur of the moment. That, after all, is part of the art of teaching.

We stand a better chance of getting these decisions right if we are aware of our own practices and our reasons for using them. When it comes to using learners' own language in English classes, it seems that we are less aware than we need to be. Classroom research suggests that English teachers regularly and substantially underestimate the extent to which they use their students' own language. We cannot be sure why this is so, but the most likely explanation is that many teachers 'suffer from a sense of guilt as they struggle to reconcile pedagogic ideals with contextual realities, leaving them feeling damned if they use L1 and damned if they do not' (Copland & Neokleous, 2011, p. 271). Throwing off the blinding guilt will be a necessary first step in being able to make informed and appropriate decisions about when and how often to use bilingual techniques.

References

Agustin Llach, M. (2009) 'The role of Spanish L1 in the Vocabulary Use of CLIL and non-CLIL EFL Learners' in Ruiz de Zarobe, Y. & Jimenez Catalan, R. M. (eds.) *Content and Language Integrated Learning*, Bristol: Multilingual Matters, pp. 112–19.

Cameron, L. (2001) *Teaching Languages to Young Learners*, Cambridge: Cambridge University Press.

Copland, F. & Neokleous, G. (2011) 'L1 to teach L2: complexities and contradictions' *ELT Journal* 65/3, pp. 270–80. Available online by subscription at: http://eltj.oxfordjournals.org/content/65/3/270.full. [Last accessed 01 July 2013]

Moon, J. (2000) *Children Learning English*, Oxford: Macmillan Heinemann.

2.1 Sandwiching

It is quite possible that you have used the technique of sandwiching without knowing its name.

When you are speaking to the class, or an individual student, in English, insert a translation into the students' own language of a word or phrase of anything that you think is important, but that you think may be difficult for the students to understand. Immediately after this own-language gloss, repeat the word or phrase in English. Teachers can signal this sandwiching by using a short pause and lower pitch, much like an aside in a play.

Here is an example (with French):

*When you are speaking to the students, in English, and you need to say something that you think they will find difficult to understand, you insert a translation – **vous ajoutez ou insérez une traduction** – you insert a translation into the students' mother tongue, and then follow this immediately by repeating the word or phrase in English.*

Sandwiching can be useful for students of all levels and can be used at any moment in a lesson. Most typically it is used when giving instructions (see also Technique 2.2: *Giving instructions*) or when glossing a word or phrase during an explanation. It may also be used during more informal moments when, for example, the teacher is chatting with the class. Cameron (2001, p. 206) gives the following example of sandwiching in a class in Malaysia while the teacher is giving instructions.

T: *OK (.) now group one (.) say a word that you do not understand (.)* **perkataan yang kamu tak faham** *...* (Translation = *a word that you do not understand*)

T: *now (.) when I point to the word I want you to put up your hand and say the word (.) OK?* **sebut perkatataannya** (Translation = *say the word*)

This technique allows teachers to introduce new language in a meaningful and gradual way without breaking up the flow of the lesson. In the process, a large number of both planned and incidental opportunities for learning can be created. Butzkamm & Caldwell (2009) have argued that this technique is the single most important technique in foreign language teaching, but remind the reader that it has nothing to do with the practice of some teachers who translate everything that they fear students may not understand. Our aim is to work towards a policy of English only in language for classroom management and explanation. Worried that this is unachievable, many teachers never attempt it. The sandwiching technique is the most efficient way of moving towards this goal.

Multilingual contexts: see page 10
This technique cannot be used with Type A or B classes.

References

Butzkamm, W. & Caldwell, J.A.W. (2009) *The Bilingual Reform: a paradigm shift in foreign language teaching*, Tübingen: Narr Studienbücher.

Cameron, L. (2001) *Teaching Languages to Young Learners*, Cambridge: Cambridge University Press.

2.2 Giving instructions

As discussed in the previous section (2.1: *Sandwiching*), the sandwich technique will be invaluable in giving instructions for activities in the classroom. With lower-level classes, use of this technique will allow you to move gradually towards much greater use of English in classroom management and instructions.

With lower levels or with classes that are not used to studying English with English as the language of instruction, introduce basic classroom language (e.g. *Work in pairs; Compare your answers; Match the pictures to the words*) with this technique. After a while, of course, the sandwiched translations can be dropped.

Teachers with four, five or more classes in a week will find it hard to keep track of which language they have used with which class. Instead of relying on your memory and intuition, it will help to approach this in an organised way.

Keep a record of the language of instructions that you have introduced in this way. This can be done in the course of the lesson by jotting things down on a sheet of paper that can be kept with your lesson plans or administrative paperwork for the class. Add to the stock of useful words and phrases every four or five lessons.

The number of words that are needed to give instructions is relatively small, and you should be able to move quite quickly away from the need to sandwich them. The examples of rubrics in the box below are all for vocabulary exercises and they cover most task types. The language needed for other activities (reading, listening, grammar focus, etc.) often differs in only a few small details.

Match the words in the box to the definitions.
Complete the sentences with a word from the box.
Label the picture with the words in the box.
Match the pictures with the words in the box.
Look at XXX. Match the words in bold to the definitions below.
Match the words from column A with words from column B.
Replace the words in italics with a word from the box.
Choose the correct words to complete the sentences.
Complete the sentences with the correct word.
Complete the words by putting vowels (a, e, i, o, u) in the spaces.
Put the words in the box into three groups.
Put the text in the correct order.
Complete the sentences in column A with a phrase from column B.
Use a dictionary to check your answers.
Listen to the recording to check your answers.
Work in pairs. Compare your answers to exercise X.
Work in pairs. Ask and answer the questions in exercise X.
Work in pairs. Do you agree or disagree with the sentences in exercise X?
Change the sentences in exercise X so that they are true for you.

When your students no longer need sandwiched translations for the key vocabulary, you can begin to add other language that will be useful for them. You can, for example, introduce politer question forms, simple discourse markers or expressions for giving advice. These will typically be chunks of language: there is no need to wait until you have formally taught these items before introducing them. In this way, substantial amounts of language can be learned by students in an almost incidental way. The box below gives examples of the sorts of items you could introduce.

OK, everyone …
So/Right …
Could/Can you …
Try to …
I'd like you to … / I want you to …
If you want, you can …
OK, now it's time to …
OK, the next thing is to …
What I want you to do is …
What you're going to do is …
Do this on your own.
You can work with a partner, if you like/want.
OK, let's start / get going / see how quickly you can do this.

I suggested earlier that it would be useful to keep a record of language that has been introduced through sandwiching. It would be equally useful for the students to have some sort of record. This would serve two purposes: for the student, providing further exposure to the language (this time in written form) and further opportunities for memorisation; for the teacher, as a way of accelerating the process of moving away from the need to sandwich.

Keep a record of the language presented in your instructions in the form of a poster that is displayed on a wall of the classroom. This should record both the English phrase and the translation into the students' own language. You could ask or nominate a member of the class to maintain this record.

These posters work best when the phrases and their translations are written on pieces of paper that can be attached temporarily to the poster paper or wall, rather than written directly onto the poster paper. In this way, you will have a lot more flexibility.

- Phrases can be removed when they are no longer needed, and new ones added.
- The translations can be jumbled up (so that students will need to do a little more work!).
- The translations can be removed entirely. Figure 2.1 on page 24 illustrates these options in German.

English-only posters that provide useful classroom language for the students are a common feature in language classrooms. Many of the major publishing houses produce such posters from time to time, and distribute them as promotional material. These can provide a useful counterpart to posters displaying teacher language. They can also be easily adapted to be bilingual and flexible.

Figure 2.1: Jumbled bilingual instructions

Variations on bilingual instruction-giving

1 Students repeat or summarise in their own language

As an intermediary stage between sandwiched instructions and English-only, a further bilingual technique may be used. This is especially useful when longer instructions for a relatively complicated activity need to be given.

> Give instructions in English. Before asking the students to begin the activity, ask or nominate one student to repeat these in their own language, either in full or summarised form. Make sure that, over a period of time, different students have the opportunity to do this work.

Besides ensuring that everybody knows what to do, there are further advantages to this technique, as Lynne Cameron points out. The pupil who replies is doing some useful language work, and pupils who did not understand have a further chance. If this is a regular pattern in classroom talk, pupils will listen more carefully to the teacher's instructions, not only to know what to do, but also to get a turn at translating. This small change in the dynamics of micro-level talk could have an impact on learning in the longer term (Cameron, 2001, p. 206).

2   Faulty instructions

It is important to ring the changes to classroom routines, in order to keep students 'on their toes', so you may want to experiment with the following variations. The first possibility is for the teacher to provide a gloss (in the students' own language) of the instructions. However, before doing this, tell the class that you will repeat the instructions in their language, but that you will change one important detail. The students' task is to listen and identify this detail. Elicit ideas from the class, ensure that everyone is clear about what they must do, and continue with the activity.

3   Students translate instructions into English

A second variation of this technique is to give the instructions first in the students' own language, and then ask or nominate a student to repeat them in English. This is more challenging and involves 'display' language, but it provides learning opportunities and may help in edging the class towards a policy of English only.

Multilingual contexts: see page 10

Even if the teacher cannot use sandwiched instructions, it makes good sense to self-monitor the use of instructional and classroom management language. If this is introduced carefully, students can be provided with written records of this language. If they wish, they could, as homework, prepare their own translations of these. English-only classroom posters of this language will act as useful reminders.

Variation 1 of this technique can be used in Type B classes. Instead of nominating individual students to repeat or summarise the instructions in their own language, you could ask them to do this in pairs or small groups. Variations 2 and 3 are not possible with Type A or Type B classes.

Reference

Cameron, L. (2001) *Teaching Languages to Young Learners*, Cambridge: Cambridge University Press.

2.3 Own-language moments

Speaking or listening to another language can be very tiring, especially if your level of proficiency is low. There often comes a point when you simply switch off and give up. If, on top of the tiredness, you are not particularly motivated in the first place and your mind is on other things, the switching-off point can come very quickly. All teachers experience moments in their classes when students switch off. But for teachers who are teaching exclusively or predominantly through English, these moments are even more problematic, since the lack of communication between them and their students can become total. The students will not say anything (or only very little) in English, and they will understand little or nothing of what the teacher or other students are saying. Nothing of value can take place. When this happens, there is no point in persevering in English.

There will be times, then, when it will be necessary to switch away from English to another language that the students understand better. This may be the students' own language, but it might also be another shared language (for example, the language of the country in which the students are studying, even though that is not their first language). In some mixed-language classes, it will be necessary to divide students into groups with a shared language where the collective proficiency level is higher than it is in English.

Apart from moments such as these when the teaching breaks down, there will be other moments when it may be useful to use the students' own language. These will be discussed below, but the basic approach is the same.

Announce to the class that the normal English-only rule is suspended. Tell them approximately how long this will last. In most cases, this is likely to be for only a few minutes. In some classes, you may simply want to give the students a break and allow them to chat about anything they like. In other classes, you may want to set them a task which they can do in their own language. Of course, if some students prefer to continue in English, so much the better!

You might also encourage your students to move into code-switching mode (where they mix up English and their own language), rather than switching entirely into their own language. While some students will not take up this option, others will. For those that do, there is an added opportunity to experiment and explore in English without the pressure of having to use English only. For more on code-switching, see Technique 2.5: *Recasting*.

When and why own-language moments may be appropriate

The examples below are intended to be illustrative. They should be taken as moments when a teacher might *consider* an own-language moment, not as instances of moments when the students' own language is absolutely necessary.

Before speaking activities

It can be hard enough trying to speak another language without having to think about what you want to say at the same time. It is common practice for many teachers to give their students some preparation time before speaking tasks, usually in pairs or small groups (although it can also be done silently and individually), so they have time to plan or brainstorm the content of what they will say. Sometimes, this planning and brainstorming will work better if students can use their own language. It is certainly worth experimenting with the technique. A minute or two of stress-free own-language discussion may result in substantially extended English speaking. If you cannot see a payoff when the students are involved in the speaking task itself, it has cost very little to carry out the experiment.

During speaking activities

On occasion, students simply get tired when they are speaking English. Concentrating hard on trying to express themselves in the foreign language, they may be unable to concentrate on the ideas they wish to express, or they forget what they had planned to say. In order to get the activity working again, it may be enough to give the students a minute or two to take a breath and take stock in their own language, before returning to English.

After speaking activities

After a speaking activity, you may want to conduct feedback with the class about how the activity went. This may be done with the whole class or in pairs / small groups. It is an opportunity to discuss what they found easy or difficult, how successfully they completed the task, or whether they found it interesting or useful. Discussions such as these can be extremely valuable for both teacher and students, and, with lower levels, will probably need to be carried out in the students' own language. One way of focusing this kind of discussion is to ask the students to compare the way that the activity actually went with how they anticipated the activity would go while they were involved in the brainstorming stage.

Before or after language focus activities

Before an activity where students will focus on a set of vocabulary, it is often a good idea to find out what they know first. Some teachers will put their students into pairs or small groups, and ask them to go through the list to identify the words they know. In a monolingual group, we should not be too surprised if students do this by sharing translations of the items. That is, after all, how most people measure their knowledge of words in other languages, even though this measure may be less than adequate. In the interests of economy, clarity and, possibly, inevitability, there will be times when it makes sense for teachers to give the green light to quick translations of this kind. If the students' work is closely monitored, the teacher will be able to identify any false friends or other confusions.

In a similar way, at the end of a vocabulary focus activity, it may be useful to give the class a few minutes, working in pairs or groups, to check they have understood and can remember the words they have just encountered. Again, this could be done very quickly with lower levels with reference to the students' own language.

In lessons with a grammar focus, a teacher may also want to find out about what their students already know. This is probably best done with a task which will require them to use the target language, but there is a place, too, for investigating students' declarative knowledge of grammatical rules. With lower-level classes who do not know grammatical terminology in English, this will have to be done in their own language. If the lesson does contain a focus on declarative knowledge of grammar rules (and especially if the teacher has explained the grammar in the students' own language), a useful follow-up task is for the students, in pairs, to explain these rules as if they were explaining to a student from another class who has not yet studied this grammar point.

Before or after work with texts (reading and listening)

Suggestions for own-language moments for these stages of a lesson can be found in Chapter 6.

Talking about learning

Educational authorities (such as ministries), as well as individual institutions and teachers, often prioritise other curricular objectives in addition to English language learning. These may relate to notions of lifelong learning and learner autonomy (as outlined, for example, in the Common European Framework of Reference for Languages). Classroom activities which foreground these objectives include discussions of learning styles and strategies, self-evaluation, learner training and feedback on the course. Some examples of activities which encourage learners to reflect on the language of instruction can be in Chapter 3. With lower-level learners, curricular objectives of this kind may be better achieved if activities are conducted in their own language.

Developing intercultural awareness

Intercultural awareness (like learner autonomy) is a curricular objective in many teaching contexts. Sometimes, it is separate from language classes, as in some high schools in Brussels, for example, where students may spend an entire school year studying the culture of their third foreign language before they actually study the language at all. More frequently, intercultural awareness is taught alongside a language. In order for the development of intercultural awareness not to be constrained by language limitations, own-language moments will be necessary, especially with lower-level learners.

Disciplining and delicate moments

There will be moments in all classes when administrative details need to be discussed. If these are at all important, they will need to be discussed in the students' own language if the students' level is low. The same holds true for any moments when a teacher needs to align herself with the class. Examples of this kind include the imparting of sad news or the sharing of extra-curricular problems. Disciplinary talk, too, is often better done in the students' language, not only for reasons of clarity, but also for emphasis.

Practicalities

However much we might like to plan the details of our teaching, much of what we do will come in response to unplanned things that happen in the classroom. Some own-language moments (such as brainstorming and content-planning before a speaking activity) can be anticipated; others will seem like a good idea at the time. Whether these moments are planned or not, it is important that students are aware of their purpose. This will often be self-evident, but on occasion it may be helpful to explain why you want them to do something in a particular way.

It is important, too, that students are aware of the 'rules': how long the moment will last and what they will be expected to do afterwards.

The beginning and duration of an own-language moment can be clearly signalled by the teacher in a number of ways. Some teachers use a symbol (such as a flag) which is displayed for the duration of the moment. Teachers of younger learners sometimes use a pair of dolls or figurines: when one is visible, only English can be spoken; with the other, students can speak their own language. Scrivener (2012, p. 216) suggests using red and green traffic light symbols. An amber light could indicate the intermediary situation of code-switching allowed.

If, as will often be the case, these moments involve pair or group work, the teacher will probably want to move away from the front of the classroom so that they can better monitor what the students are saying. Even if it is not possible, because of the size of the room, for the teacher to move around the class, it may be a good idea to stand or sit in a different place. When you then move back to the place where you habitually sit or stand, this will signal to the class that the own-language moment is over.

An indication of the length of the own-language moment will also be useful. The length will depend on a number of factors. In some lower-level classes, you are perhaps more likely to indicate English-only moments than own-language moments. Giving time limits can help to focus the students' attention on the task at hand. It is inevitable that the teacher will not always stick rigidly to the time limit.

Finally, you might like to experiment with allowing the class more of a say in what language is allowed. Ideally, our learners would be sufficiently self-aware, responsible and sophisticated as learners to know when they would benefit more from speaking one language or the other. As a step in this direction, some teachers operate a system like a basketball game where students themselves can call a certain number of own-language timeouts (five or six, for example, in a forty-five minute period) in the course of a lesson.

Multilingual contexts: see page 10

Own-language moments can be used very productively in Type B classes if the students are organised into appropriate groups. Teachers who cannot understand the other language(s) are clearly at a disadvantage, but, assuming that discipline is not an issue, there may be no particular reason for the teacher to understand what is being said.

Reference

Scrivener, J. (2012) *Classroom Management Techniques*, Cambridge: Cambridge University Press.

2.4 Language monitoring

There will be times when learners want to express something, do not have the English to do so and cannot refrain from using their own language. The instinct of most teachers is to treat these moments as unwelcome, but an alternative view is to consider them occasionally as a potential resource.

If a student lapses into their own language, the teacher has five options:

- Encourage the student to recast the sentence in English.
- Elicit a recasting in English from another student.
- Recast it personally.
- Say nothing but make a note of it.
- Ignore it.

The first two options will take the longest and will break up the flow of the lesson most. If you want to keep things moving, this is a problem. We will look at teacher recasting in the next section of this chapter (2.5: *Recasting*). In this section, we will consider the possibility of taking notes.

At any moment of the lesson, when a student says something in their own language and you do not want to stop the lesson to deal with it, make a note of it. Ignore very low-frequency words that are unlikely to be useful later. You could make these notes on a piece of paper or quickly scribble them on one side of the board. At the end of the lesson, dictate these words and phrases (in the students' language) or direct students' attention to the items on the board. Then, put students into pairs or small groups and ask them to discuss how these items could be expressed in English. You may wish to allow them to use dictionaries. After they have had enough time to do this work, conduct feedback with the whole class. During this stage, ask the students if they can remember the context in which the words or phrases were used earlier in the lesson.

Taking notes while continuing to teach the class is not easy. It is a skill that requires practice. Fortunately, there is an alternative, and it is one with even richer potential.

Nominate a student to act as language monitor. Their task is to note down anything that is said in students' own language at moments when everyone should be trying to speak in English. This may be individual words or short phrases – see the example opposite (Figure 2.2) from a class in Austria, which includes an expression partly in English and partly in German. This technique works particularly well when students are working in groups and there is one language monitor for each group. At the end of the activity, the language monitor shows the other members of the group what they have noted down. The members of the group work together to discuss how these things might have been said in English. This can be followed by whole-class feedback. Data collected in this way can also be saved, and exploited in a subsequent lesson.

Using a student as a language monitor during group work often encourages the other members of the group to monitor their own language more. It can motivate them to work harder to express their ideas in English. What often happens in practice is that, during the group work, students will help and correct each other more than would normally be the case. The technique also works to draw students' attention, first, to the fact that they can learn from each other and, second, that they have more language resources than they can access at any given moment.

Figure 2.2: Student's handwritten notes

You can also ask for students to volunteer for this role, although it is important, of course, that it is not always the same person. However, if you decide to nominate a student yourself, how do you choose? You might select a student who would otherwise dominate the group work, if you make it clear that the role is purely that of observer/listener, and not participant. You might, equally, select a student whose level of English is so much lower than the others that there is a very strong chance they will say nothing at all during the activity. At least, in this way, they are encouraged to listen to what is being said. There will be other reasons, in any class, for nominating other students. As you use this technique, you will discover which students can carry out the role effectively. It presupposes a degree of maturity and cooperation and should not be used as a reward or a punishment.

Multilingual contexts: see page 10
Language monitoring can be used in Type B classes. Teachers who cannot speak the students' language(s) cannot do the monitoring themselves, but students can perform this role. When the time comes to look at the own-language moments that have been recorded, the class or the group can look at these independently of the teacher. Teachers will want, however, as part of their own development, to note the kinds of language that have been recorded.

2.5 Recasting

When a learner code-switches, your response will be determined, in part, by your understanding of the reasons for this code-switching, and, in part, by your priorities at that moment of the lesson. Some teachers will try to insist that the student makes an effort to express their ideas, however imperfectly, in English. Some will try to elicit an English version from other members of the class. Some will pretend that they do not understand what the student has said, but I have rarely seen this work effectively when everybody knows that there is a shared language. All of this takes time, and there are many classroom moments when we want to move on quickly and not distract from our primary focus. Recasting the student's utterance is a simple way to do this.

Indicate that you have understood what a student has said in their own language by reformulating it in English.

Read (2007, p. 18) gives the following example from a class of young learners, but the technique is equally useful with adults.

S: *Mira! El monkey está allí* (Translation = *Look! The monkey's there*).
T: *Yes, you're right. The monkey's there.*

In this example, the teacher probably does not want to dampen youthful enthusiasm. With more adult classes, we may also wish to maintain a positive atmosphere, but we may expect our students to be a little more self-conscious in their choice of language! The most appropriate moments for recasting are those when students are making an effort to express themselves in English, but lack a word or phrase which they need.

This will often happen in language-focus parts of the lesson. In the example below, from a class in Hungary, the teacher is getting the students to practise using the present perfect simple in basic questions and answers. The student, Csaba, wants to say more than just a short answer (*Yes, I have.* / *No, I haven't.*)

T: *So, Csaba, have you ever been to England?*
S: *No, I have never been to ... külföldön* (Translation = *abroad*), *but I'd like it.*
T: *So, you have never been abroad. How about you, Orsi? Have you ever been to London? ...*

It is generally agreed that there is a value in encouraging our students to express personal meanings, and personalised grammar and vocabulary practice is becoming increasingly common. If we genuinely want our students to say something that they actually mean, rather than restricting themselves to what they can actually say in English, we must accept that code-switching will take place. The next example is from a low-level class in Romania that is practising simple past with time adverbials.

S: *Last Sunday we went to ... Gradina Zoologica.* (Translation = *zoo*)
T: *Oh, you went to the zoo. Interesting. Did you have a good time at the zoo?*

In addition to such language-focused moments, teachers can use recasting as a way of encouraging English use at other, less formal moments. In the following example, the teacher recasts what has been said in Hungarian, and then throws it back as a question so that the student has a chance to repeat, in a meaningful way, the word that they were lacking.

S: *Sorry, Mr Lorincz, that I am late, but I lekéstem a buszt.* (Translation = *I missed the bus*)
T: *So, you missed the bus. And how did you miss the bus? How did you manage to miss the bus?*

If you think that a student knows the English words for what they have expressed in their own language, you may, as an alternative to providing a full recast in English yourself, give a partial recast only. For individual words, this could be the first syllable or the first consonant. For a longer phrase, you could provide the first few words and invite the student to complete it.

Multilingual contexts: see page 10

This technique cannot be used in Type A classes. Although it might be possible to use pairs and groups for recasting work in Type B classes where there is only one shared language, this is likely to break up the flow of the lesson too much.

Reference

Reed, C. (2007) *500 Activities for the Primary Classroom*, Oxford: Macmillan Education.

2.6 Own-language mirroring

Mirroring is an adaptation of literal translation (see also Activity 7.11: *Word-for-word translation*). The term 'mirroring' was coined by Butzkamm & Caldwell (2009, pp. 106–11), who described the technique as '"frenchifying" or "germanising" English, "anglicising" French, etc.' As a way of drawing learners' attention to the problems of language transfer (also known as 'L1 interference') in a quick and memorable way, it is a powerful technique indeed.

> When you hear an error which you think has been caused by language transfer, give a literal translation of the incorrect word or phrase. This should make it absolutely clear to the class that there is a language transfer problem.

The easiest way of using this technique is with false friends (see also Activities 7.3: *False friends*, and 7.4: *False friends revision*). In the example below, the student is talking about plans for the evening and the teacher suspects that there has been a confusion between *eventually* and the Romanian word *eventual*.

S: *Eventually, we could pick her up on our way to the cinema.*
T: *Eventually? 'În cele din urmă'? Is that what you mean? Because if you don't, you'll need a different word there. How about 'maybe' or 'perhaps'?*

Mirroring can also be used for correction of written work. In the example below (Figure 2.3), the student has made two common mistakes. Judging by the level of the rest of the writing here, the student could almost certainly correct his or her own mistakes. The teacher has chosen to highlight the problems by using the student's own language, German. As a correction technique, it is clear and economical, but it still requires the student to do some thinking.

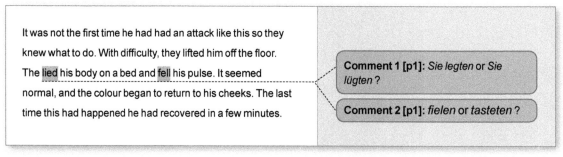

Figure 2.3: Error correction technique

Own-language mirroring also has potential for humour. In the following example, the teacher could have corrected the error in English, but chose a combination of English and the shared language of Romanian to ensure that everyone got the joke.

S: *She is really beautiful. She's tall and slim and she has blue eyes and a long hair.*
T: *A hair? One single hair? Un fir de păr? Un singur fir de păr?*

In another class the same teacher picked up on the following pronunciation error. Not wanting to translate *bitches* into Romanian herself, she nevertheless made it clear that the students should figure out the translation for themselves. She used the shared language, raised eyebrows and a wide grin to make the point as saliently as possible.

> S: *I would like to spend my holidays on the bitches in Brazil.*
> T: *Nu cred ca asta e ce vrei sa spui ... I don't think that's what you mean to say ... Careful with the pronunciation: it's 'beaches' you wanted to say, isn't it?*

When teaching French, I have had similar fun in classes where students are struggling with French vowel sounds, especially /u/ and /y/ as in the words *cou* (neck) and *cul* (backside). Humour can be very useful when it comes to raising our learners' language awareness.

In all the examples above, mirroring has been used for correction, but Butzkamm and Caldwell's main recommendation is to use the technique for clarification of the surface structure of new language. They advise against overuse, but occasional employment can be a very memorable way of highlighting grammatical forms.

> When presenting new language where the surface structure does not correspond to the surface structure of the equivalent phrase in the students' own language, give the students a literal translation.

In the example below, the teacher is drawing students' attention to a dependent preposition (*depend + on*) which she knows is often a problem for speakers of French. She stresses the incorrect French preposition in the mirrored translation. There is no danger that the students will start making mistakes in their own language: it is precisely because *dépend sur* is and sounds so wrong that she hopes to make the English form more memorable.

> T: *It depends on what you mean. Depends **on**. Ça dépend **sur** ce que vous voulez dire. Depends **on**.*

In a similar way, when introducing the phrase *on my/his/her/your own*, the teacher provides an over-literal translation with the intention of making the English expression both salient and memorable.

> T: *He did it on his own. Il l'a fait tout seul. Il l'a fait sur son propre! On his own. He did it on his own.*

The power of such mirroring, which can often be funny, is well illustrated by the title of the best-selling French book by Jean-Loup Chiflet, *Sky my Husband! Guide of the Running English!* (*Ciel mon mari! Guide de l'anglais courant*).

> **Multilingual contexts: see page 10**
> This technique cannot be used with Type A or B classes.

References

Butzkamm, W. & Caldwell, J.A.W. (2009) *The Bilingual Reform: a paradigm shift in foreign language teaching*, Tübingen: Narr Studienbücher.

Chiflet, J.-L. (1994) *Ciel mon Mari! Sky my Husband!*, Paris: Seuil.

2.7 Wall displays

When lessons regularly take place in the same room (and when institutional regulations permit), it is a good idea to use the wall space to make for a rich linguistic environment. It is common practice for teachers to display posters that have been professionally produced by publishing companies and tourist agencies. These can be modified with bilingual elements or usefully supplemented by home-produced materials. Here are some suggestions:

- for lower-level classes, lists of useful 'classroom language' phrases with own-language equivalents
- lists of false friends
- lists of true friends/cognates
- lists of true friends/cognates with information about pronunciation issues (different word stress patterns, or phonemic differences)
- bilingual mind maps of lexical sets
- annotated examples of amusing bad translations from English into students' own language (see Activity 7.8: *Street English*)
- collections of annotated and corrected examples of student-generated language where own-language interference is a problem (e.g. from students' written work)
- lyrics of English-language pop songs and poems with own-language translations
- collections of inspiring or amusing quotations with translations
- poster displays about different dictionaries (both print and online), with recommendations
- poster displays of popular or useful English-language websites, with own-language annotations and tips
- information about useful online resources (e.g. online translation tools, sites offering subtitled video streaming, sites with bilingual song lyrics, downloadable apps such as bilingual word cards).

Notes

1 For many of these ideas, students (either individually or in groups) can be asked to collect the data themselves, as part of their homework.
2 In some of the suggestions above, the posters should be 'unfinished' and should be added to when appropriate.
3 Change classroom posters regularly. They will have much more impact if you do.

Multilingual contexts: see page 10

If there is a manageable number of own-languages in the class, there is no reason not to encourage the production of different versions of wall posters. Even if, say, an English–Polish display may not especially contribute to the English language learning of, say, a Chinese learner in the class, it may be *interesting*. It might also contribute to insights about languages, language differences and other cultures. In some educational contexts, this is an important part of the curriculum.

3 Attitudes

Strength of feelings

The use of the student's own language is a very hot potato in language teaching. Thornbury (2013) has claimed that no other issue has so polarised opinion in the field. In some institutions, it is completely banned and teachers can lose their jobs if they are caught transgressing. The strength of feeling is, however, mostly one-sided: until very recently, the voice of disapproval has been rather louder than the voice of acceptance.

One of the main problems in this debate is that a number of issues have been conflated. In the minds of some, any mention of own-language use evokes the word 'translation', even if translation is just one instance of own-language use. 'Translation' has become a taboo word in language teaching. For example, Goldstein (2010) has described how he incorporated elements of contrastive analysis (see Chapter 7) in one series of books. When it was time for a second edition of the books to be prepared, these elements remained, but he was instructed to change the rubrics in order to eliminate the word 'translation' by using paraphrases such as 'How would you say this in your language?'. It was not the idea, he said, 'but the "t" word which was considered taboo'.

Translation suffers because it is associated with grammar-translation, which is sometimes portrayed as representing everything that is bad about language teaching. However, criticisms of grammar-translation have tended to focus selectively on a limited number of the techniques of this approach. A fair evaluation will only be possible if there is further research into the relative effectiveness of grammar-translation and the more communicative approaches that came after it.

There is a wide spectrum of uses of the learner's own language in language teaching, ranging from occasional clarification of meaning to running the whole lesson. There is also an important difference between teacher and learner use of this language. In the criticisms of translation/own-language use, there is rarely much attention to details and own-language moments are not differentiated adequately. Instead, own-language moments are regarded as if they are all serving the same purpose.

The idea that we best learn another language in the same way that we learned our first language as an infant is widespread, but it is questionable. The popularity of the related idea that the best teacher is a native-speaker teacher (who does not speak your own language) is attested to by the commercial success of large numbers of private language schools around the world that employ predominantly or exclusively native-speaker teachers. There are powerful vested interests in the debate about own-language use, and the assumed desirability of English-only has been little questioned until recently. The result, for many teachers, has been that the use of the students' own language has become a taboo subject and its potential as a learning and teaching resource has been 'cramped and distorted by the guilt and prohibitions that have accompanied its use' (Prodromou, 2002, p. 5).

Changing attitudes

The strength of feeling is such, in some contexts, that individual teachers or trainers may need to tread a very careful path. Most educational change is slow and incremental, rather than brought about by sudden flashes of theoretical insight. For learners, a greater awareness of themselves as learners may lead to a re-evaluation of preferences and learning strategies, and the first three activities in this chapter are intended to bring the question of own-language use to the foreground. At the same time, a more developed understanding of the learning tools that are available to them (e.g. dictionaries, websites) may also result in a shift in attitude. These will be the subject of Chapter 4. Equally importantly, it should not be too difficult to demonstrate that activities which involve the students' own language can provide real learning gains, and that they do not need to be of the dry and dusty 'Who-will-translate-the-next-line?' approach.

The appendix of this book contains three activities which are intended to address the issue of own-language use in the context of teacher training and teacher development contexts. These should be considered as only a starting point. Teachers, like learners, tend to change their practices slowly and incrementally, and it is probably through the process of trying things out, of finding what 'works', that development takes place most lastingly. Alongside such work in the training room, teachers should be encouraged to experiment with techniques and activities in their classrooms piecemeal (especially the basic techniques in Chapter 2).

Institutional constraints and policies cannot, however, be neglected. Senior members of staff, such as department heads, who have spent a lifetime believing that English-only is the only way, will be very resistant to change. Small-scale action research programmes will perhaps be one way of moving towards change, but, at some point, institutional educational policies will need to be examined and revised. There is nothing so hard to change as common-sense, received wisdom, even when it is misinformed!

The last activity in this chapter is rather different from the others, which encourage learners to reflect on the respective uses of English and their own languages in their learning of English. This activity is intended for use in classes where there is no shared language other than English, and provides students with the opportunity to teach a little of their own language to the rest of the class. To do so, they will only be able to use English.

References

Goldstein, B. (2010) Post on Thornbury, S. (2010) 'G is for Grammar-Translation' in *An A–Z of ELT* (blog 15 October 2010). Available online at: http://scottthornbury.wordpress.com/2010/10/15/g-is-for-grammar-translation/. [Last accessed 01 July 2013]

Prodromou, L. (2002) Introduction to Deller, S. & M. Rinvolucri, *Using the Mother Tongue*, Peaslake, Surrey: Delta Publishing.

Thornbury, S. (2013) *Big Questions in ELT*, The Round ebook, www.the-round.com.

3.1 Questionnaire: own-language use in the classroom

Outline	Students discuss their previous English learning experiences and their teachers' use of the students' own language.
Level	A2+ (adult learners)
Time	Approximately 30 minutes
Preparation	Make a sufficient number of copies of the questionnaire for the class to work in pairs or small groups. Alternatively, the questionnaire can be projected onto the board or wall. You may want to add or edit some questions. With lower-level classes, you will need to translate the questionnaire into the students' own language.

Procedure

1 Distribute the questionnaire. Students work in pairs or small groups and discuss their answers. (There is no need to write anything down.)
2 When the students have had enough time to discuss their answers to the questions, ask them to spend a few minutes preparing a summary of what they have discussed.
3 Ask or nominate individual students to summarise their discussions. Conduct feedback with the whole of the class.

Notes

1 This activity will be particularly suitable for groups of students who are beginning a course, especially if they are just starting in a new institution (e.g. a language school or the first year of university) where approaches to teaching may be different from those previously experienced.
2 The primary purpose of the activity is to raise awareness of these issues. Lower-level students can speak their own language, but with those students whose English is of a sufficiently high level, the activity can be considered as an opportunity for fluency practice. Even with lower-level students, the reporting stage could be done in English.
3 With less mature students, it may be necessary to point out that you are not interested in gossip or slander about other teachers. Point out that the subject of the discussion is the use of their own language in the English classroom, not the personalities of individual teachers.
4 You may wish to follow up this activity with Activity 3.2: *Language rules*.
5 In institutions which have an English-only policy, you will need to think carefully before using this activity. Given the strength of feeling about such policies in some contexts, you may run the risk of offending sensibilities.

Multilingual contexts: see page 10

It is probably impractical to arrange for the translation of the questionnaire into many different languages (necessary for low level groups) with Type A classes. Since, too, in a class of this type, the use of the students' own languages is necessarily very limited, the issues addressed by the questionnaire and discussion are of limited relevance.

In Type B classes, students can use dictionaries to help in their understanding of the questionnaire, they can be arranged into own-language groups for the discussion (if necessary), and feedback can be done in English if sufficient time is provided to prepare for this.

Questionnaire: using your own language in the classroom

1 How many different teachers of English have you had in your life? When and how often did your previous teachers use your own language? Tick the boxes.

	always	sometimes	occasionally	never
a giving instructions and managing the class				
b disciplining the class				
c chatting with the class				
d explaining grammar or vocabulary				
e correcting				
f checking the class has understood a reading or listening exercise				
g in tests and exams				
h helping individual students				

2 Do you think that it is better for a teacher to use your own language or only English for activities a–h above? Why?

3 Which do you think is better? Why?

☐ to study English in a class where all the students (and the teacher) speak your language

☐ to study English in a class where all the students speak different languages (and the teacher only speaks English)

3.2 Language rules

Outline	Students discuss the use of their own language in the classroom, and the class works towards agreeing a 'class contract'.
Level	A2+
Time	Approximately 30 minutes
Preparation	Make a sufficient number of copies of the 'rules' for the class to work in small groups. Alternatively, the questionnaire can be projected onto the board or wall. Handout A can be used with students whose level is B2 or above. Handout B can be used with B1 groups. For very low-level groups, you may need to simplify Handout B further, provide a glossary or translate it.

Procedure

1 Distribute the handout. Give the class enough time to read the text silently: seven or eight minutes should be enough. (If more time is needed, it is better to simplify the language or translate it, in advance, into the students' own language). Check that everyone has understood everything and answer any queries.

2 Organise the class into small groups (approximately four students per group). Tell the groups to work through the points on the handout, evaluating each suggestion and deciding whether it would be an appropriate policy for their class. Tell them to use English as much as possible, but point out that, for this activity, their ideas are more important than practising English.

3 Write numbers 1–11 on the board (1–8 if you are using Handout B). Ask one member from each group to come to the board and put a tick, a cross or a question mark next to each of these numbers (the numbers correspond to the points on the handout). A tick indicates that they think this is a good idea, a cross indicates that they think this is a bad idea, and a question mark indicates that the group is not sure or cannot agree.

4 Discuss with the whole class any of the points where students have put a cross or a question mark, or where there is a difference of opinion between groups.

5 Once the class has reached broad agreement on some or all of the points, suggest that this document will now form a 'class contract'. Make a copy of the points that have been agreed and display it on the classroom wall. Agree with the class a suitable time in the future to review the contract and how well it is working.

Note

In some contexts, students believe that the entire lesson should be conducted in English. More often, however, teachers find that one of the most challenging parts of their job is persuading the students to say *anything* in English! Weaning students onto a teaching methodology where English is the only language used will usually take time, and some students will be a lot slower than others. Patience and sensitivity are the key words.

Multilingual contexts: see page 10

The activity is not relevant for Type A classes. In Type B classes, the simplified version of the handout (Handout B) can be used and dictionaries can be used, if necessary, with lower-level groups. Students can also be arranged into own-language groups for the discussion, and feedback can be done in English if sufficient time is provided to prepare for this. Be prepared for differences of opinion between students of different learning backgrounds.

Handout A

Language rules

We all know that the more you try to use English, the more progress you will make. Sometimes there will be a good reason for using your own language in the classroom, but it's easy to become lazy.

Work in small groups and look at the ideas below. Which of these ideas do you think are good ideas for your class? Give your reasons ... and speak in English as much as you can!

1   The teacher will indicate (with a sign on the board) when (a) only English may be used, (b) the students' own language may be used, (c) both languages may be used, but English is preferable. At different moments of a lesson, different rules will apply.

2   The teacher will ignore students who speak their own language (if the teacher believes that the student was able to express the same ideas in English).

3   Individual students are allowed to use their own language a certain number of times in each lesson. This number will decrease during the academic year.

4   When students want to use their own language, they must also write down what they have said. From time to time, the teacher will use these records in class as the basis of a part of a lesson.

5   When students cannot express their ideas in English, they can ask another student for help. But they must then repeat what they want to say in English.

6   Students are evaluated on their attempts to use English. Students who make a consistent effort to speak only English receive higher grades.

7   Students are penalised when they use their own language. After a certain number of 'offences', they must 'pay a penalty' (e.g. do a chore, such as cleaning the board, or do extra homework).

8   Students must ask permission before using their own language.

9   In group work, one student is a 'language monitor', whose responsibility is to note how much students use their own language and to encourage greater use of English.

10   In group work, students audio-record their discussions. This may help to discourage own-language use, but students can also go back and listen to the recordings and identify moments when they used their own language and their reasons for doing so.

11   Students promise to make an effort; the teacher promises to be patient!

Handout B

Language rules

You want to make progress in English? Speak more English! But sometimes, there is a good reason for using your own language in the classroom ...

Work in small groups and look at the ideas below. Which ideas are good ideas for your class? Give your reasons ... and speak in English as much as you can!

1   The teacher shows (with a sign on the board) when (a) you can only speak English, (b) you can speak your own language, (c) you can speak English **or** your own language.

2   The teacher does not answer a student who speaks his/her own language ... **if** the student is able to express the same ideas in English.

3   Individual students can use their own language X times in each lesson. During the academic year, the number X gets smaller.

4   When students cannot express their ideas in English, another student can help. But they must then repeat the word or phrase in English.

5   The teacher grades the students for their **efforts** to use English.

6   The teacher penalises students when they use their own language. If students use their own language too often, they must, for example, clean the board or do extra homework.

7   Students must ask permission before they use their own language.

8   In group work, one student is a 'language monitor'. His/Her job is to note how much the other students use their own language. He/She must also encourage everyone to use English.

3.3 Same but different

Outline	Groups of students do a communicative speaking task in different ways – some using English only, others being allowed to use own language. They then discuss their different experiences.
Level	A2+ (adults)
Time	10–15 minutes
Preparation	This activity is a way of managing any communicative speaking activity where the class is working in groups. Appropriate activities include discussions and problem-solving tasks, where the focus is on speaking practice, rather than the practice of particular language items. One example of such a task is a simple ranking activity where students rank the following in terms of their importance in learning another language: memorising vocabulary, watching TV programmes in the language, spending some time in the country where the language is spoken, working with a good grammar book, etc.

Procedure

1 Set up and set the speaking task. Organise the class into groups for the activity.
2 Tell half the groups that they must speak English only. (You may find it useful to have one student in each group taking the role of 'language monitor' (see Activity 2.4: *Language monitoring*) whose task is to ensure that only English is spoken). Tell the other groups that they may use their own language when they feel it is necessary.
3 The students carry out the speaking task. Conduct any feedback (e.g. feedback on task performance, error correction, etc.) after the task as you would normally do.
4 Write the following questions on the board. With lower-level groups, it will be necessary to translate the questions into the students' own language. The students discuss these questions in their groups.

English-only groups
- When, during the activity, did you most want to use your own language?
- Do you think that other students in your group could have helped you to express your ideas (if your own language had been allowed)?
- Would other students have been able to help you to express your ideas in English if you had been able to use your own language?
- In English classes, do you think it is useful to be able to use your own language from time to time? If so, when and why?

English and own-language groups
- Did the use of your own language help you and the group to do the task? If so, in what ways?
- Did you find it easy or difficult to switch between English and your own language?
- In English classes, do you think it is useful to be able to use your own language from time to time? If so, when and why?

5   Rearrange the groups so that the new groups are composed equally of students from the original English-only and the English + own-language groups. Students report back on their previous discussions and compare their answers. With low-level classes, the students should speak their own language.

6   Conduct feedback with the whole class.

Multilingual contexts: see page 10

The activity is not relevant for Type A classes. In Type B classes, students can be arranged into own-language groups for the speaking task. The feedback discussion between students can also be done in these language groups, but this should be summarised afterwards in English for the teacher.

3.4 Learn my language

Outline	Students teach a short dialogue in their own language to other students in the class.
Level	A2+
Time	Approximately 20 minutes
Preparation	At regular intervals throughout the course, students will teach mini-lessons in their own language to the rest of the class. Decide in advance with the individual students the dates for these presentations/mini-lessons and make sure that the students have a reasonable idea of the sort of dialogue that they could teach. You will need some A1 coursebooks, or photocopies of pages from these books, for the students to look at for ideas.

Procedure

1   Allocate some time in class for students to begin to think about their mini-lessons. The rest of the planning can be done as a homework assignment. Explain what they must do, and say that they will have 15–20 minutes in class to teach their dialogues.

Most students prefer to have some sort of model to work from. For this, find a selection of pieces of material from an A1 level coursebook (in English) which present and practise short dialogues (e.g. first introductions, in a restaurant, at a car-rental office, etc.). See the example in figure 3.1.

The students will need to plan their mini-lesson. Suggest that they begin by selecting a short dialogue, which they must translate into their own language. They then plan a variety of short activities which will lead the rest of the class to acting out the dialogue. Some students will attach a lot of importance to this task (as it is a way of showcasing their own language/culture): be prepared to help with advice and suggestions.

2   From time to time, begin lessons by asking one of the students to teach the dialogue from their language. This is better done at the start of the lesson than at the end, when there may be time pressure. Join the class yourself as one of the students.

3   When the teaching is complete, discuss the activity with the 'teacher' and the rest of the class. Ask what they found easy and difficult, and which sections of the lesson they most enjoyed.

Figure 3.1: From Redston, C. (2006) *face2face* Starter Student's Book, Cambridge: Cambridge University Press, p. 6

Multilingual contexts: see page 10

The activity is only relevant for Type A classes.

---

4   Tools

What kind of tools are there?

Digital technology has brought a huge proliferation of language learning tools. Traditional print media continue to diversify (e.g. dictionaries, magazines, graded or parallel readers), with increasing bilingual options. But almost all of the printed content is also available in other formats, for delivery to laptops, smartphones, interactive whiteboards, or learning platforms. These media also benefit from being online, where they can connect with other services, such as instant machine translation. All of the activities in this chapter encourage learners to explore the options that are available to them.

Digital literacies

Students are sometimes better informed than teachers about the tools available to them, but they do not always know how to make the best, or most critical, use of them. Our students may know their way around the Web, but they are not necessarily digitally literate. Digital literacy is being promoted by many governments around the world and is a central part of the curriculum in many educational contexts. Language teachers cannot really afford to be digitally illiterate themselves.

Many language learners will turn, outside the classroom, to digital aids and resources, even if only to do their homework more accurately or quickly. Many will be using online dictionaries, online translation tools, streamed movies and video clips with subtitles, and various apps on their smartphones. Some will be using these resources in an attempt to cheat. Learners will clearly benefit from guidance in their choice of tools, and guidance in how to use them. It may not be apparent to some that the openly-editable nature of online encyclopaedias (such as Wikipedia) means that their accuracy is not guaranteed and that an online translation tool – any online translation tool – may not be the most accurate way to translate a text.

Monolingual, bilingual or bilingualised?

Many of the learning aids available to learners and teachers come in both monolingual and bilingual versions: dictionaries, videos, websites, games, grammar guides and coursebooks often exist in two versions. For any given group of learners, which of these will be more appropriate?

Conventional teacher wisdom has tended to prefer monolingual tools. For a long time, monolingual learner's dictionaries were promoted over small bilingual dictionaries, despite the fact that most learners have repeatedly shown a preference for the latter. Research that supports the teacher's preference is, however, limited. Hayati & Fattahzadeh (2006, p. 125) suggested that the choice of good monolingual or good bilingual dictionary did not have any serious impact in learners' vocabulary retention. Conventional wisdom is not always supported by research evidence.

Recent and continuing developments in participatory media, including online dictionaries, have transformed the landscape so quickly that it is not easy to remain up-to-date. Both print and online dictionaries are moving on: there are now excellent bilingualised dictionaries (which combine the best features of monolingual and bilingual dictionaries), both in print and online, which are often free.

Lower-level learners, those between A1 and B1, will especially benefit from using bilingual or bilingualised resources. Most higher-level learners will have less need of them, but still find them useful sometimes. For example, small bilingual dictionaries will still be useful for reading, but of less value for writing. All learners will benefit from an awareness of the tools that are available to them, monolingual, bilingual or bilingualised. The merits and demerits of particular tools are more important than loose generalisations about language exclusion. Learners need to know about what's out there.

There are, of course, very many, very good monolingual resources, and learners should be encouraged to make use of them. With bilingual tools, it is often only the rubrics or explanations that are given in the learner's own language, and these are more of a psychological barrier than a substantial one. With a little help, most if not all monolingual tools can be made more accessible. Activity 4.12: *Using monolingual tools: making a glossary*, is one way of doing this.

Learner preferences: being online

In the same way that most learners tend to prefer bilingual resources to monolingual ones, they tend to prefer electronic/digital formats to printed ones. The two most popular online, bilingual resources are translation programs and dictionaries.

There are a number of widely used, free online translation services. Different services work more or less well with different language combinations. Some of the most well-known are:

- Google Translate: translate.google.com
- Reverso: www.reverso.net
- Bing Translator: www.bing.com/translator

As teachers, we need to know which of these services work best for the language combination we are teaching. It's worth remembering, too, that these services are in competition with each other, and the service they offer can change almost overnight.

We also need to know which dictionaries to recommend. The main monolingual dictionaries are all available in digital format, and some are free (e.g. dictionary.cambridge.org). Some also provide learner-training material and supplementary exercises. Many bilingual dictionaries are also free, or extremely cheap, as apps for smartphones, but the quality varies widely. Some language-pairings are much more common than others, and some bilingual dictionaries are now extremely good. They are usually easy to locate with a standard search engine. Teachers are usually the best judges of what is most appropriate for the students in their class.

A small number of sites offer multiple language-pairings, and can be a good place to start, especially for European languages:

- WordReference.com (www.wordreference.com) has 15 languages paired with English, at the time of writing, and links to other dictionaries (such as Collins).
- PONS.eu (en.pons.eu) has more language pairings, but primarily European ones. Based in Stuttgart, it also offers a German–Elvish dictionary, in case you need one!
- Dict.cc (www.dict.cc) has a wide number of pairings. Some (e.g. English–German) are well established; others are still under construction.
- The Cambridge online dictionary website (dictionary.cambridge.org) includes a number of specialised monolingual dictionaries (e.g. business English) and currently has two bilingual

dictionaries: English–Spanish (dictionary.cambridge.org/dictionary/english-spanish) and English–Turkish (dictionary.cambridge.org/dictionary/Turkish).

Most teachers have classroom policies on the use of laptops, phones and other devices. Sometimes these policies are part of broader institutional or even governmental policies, which may not be susceptible to change. The banning of mobile technology from the classroom completely needs to be considered in the light of what the technology can offer to promote learning and motivation. Clear policies are needed to make the most of the technology and not to allow it to become a distraction.

Print resources

Teachers usually have classroom policies concerning print resources, dictionaries, in particular. Few students like to carry around heavy books, so smaller, less comprehensive bilingual dictionaries proliferate. Few institutions can afford to have good sets of dictionaries in every classroom. Mobile technology is becoming better and more widely accepted, but print books continue to be widely used.

With limited budgets, schools and teachers need to think carefully about how to invest in classroom resources. Class sets of dictionaries (one for every two or three students in the class) are excellent, but will one set be enough for a classroom that hosts different levels? Will a monolingual or a bilingual dictionary be more popular with (a) the teachers, and (b) the students? Will the students be trained to use whatever set of dictionaries is bought? Will there be rules about when dictionaries can be consulted, and when not?

Teachers can sometimes tell their students to buy supplementary materials, such as a dictionary. Again, careful consideration is needed as the quality of print media is changing almost as fast as digital media. New products are continually being developed for English language learners, and many of these are bilingualised: vocabulary books, grammar reference and exercise books, workbooks and coursebook companions, and so on.

Learners can only benefit from knowing what is on the market, but they will need help in both choosing and using. Some of the major dictionaries are supported by free websites that provide guidance and training, and this is worth bearing in mind, both when choosing and using. Further useful classroom activities for training students in dictionary use can be found in Leaney (2007).

Other resources

In an ideal situation, learners will have individual access to online tools, but ideal situations are rare. A good alternative option is for the classroom to have a projector and laptop or interactive whiteboard (IWB), ideally online, but this is not always necessary if the teacher has, for example, prepared a slide show with screenshots or downloaded content media. If this is not possible, many activities can be set up in class, and students have to do online research / work somewhere out of the classroom.

References

Hayati, M. & Fattahzadeh, A. (2006) 'The effect of monolingual and bilingual dictionaries on vocabulary recall and retention of EFL learners' in *The Reading Matrix* Vol. 6, No. 2, pp. 125–34.

Leaney, C. (2007) *Dictionary Activities*, Cambridge: Cambridge University Press.

4.1 Using online dictionaries 1 (editing students' own work)

Outline	Students use online dictionaries to edit their own writing. They also explore and discuss their use of online dictionaries.
Level	A2+
Time	Approximately 40 minutes
Preparation	This activity is intended to be used in the context of writing skills development. After students have brainstormed ideas for producing a particular piece of writing (e.g. a narrative, an email, a composition), and after they have shaped these ideas into a plan, encourage them to write a first draft very fast. They should feel free to include elements from their own language (words and phrases), to leave blanks, to use diagrams and annotations – anything that will help them get their ideas down quickly.
	The following editing activity takes place after a very rough first draft has been produced. The students need online access to a dictionary (e.g. computers in the classroom, laptops with wifi, smartphones). See the introduction to this chapter for suggestions for online dictionaries. It is not essential that every student has individual access; groups of three will work well. If the classroom is not wired, students can also be asked to do this work as a homework assignment.

Procedure

1   Organise the class into groups of two to four students. Ask the students to look at their rough drafts in turn. They work together, using their online dictionaries and their shared ideas to improve each draft. If the piece of work is about 150 words long, they will probably need about ten minutes per draft, but this could be longer, depending on level.
2   Individual students then work another five minutes on their own draft before submitting it.
3   The teacher briefly comments on the work and uses a highlighter (either a highlighting pen, or a highlighting function on a digital document) to indicate where the student could usefully check something in the dictionary again. The work is returned to the student to write another draft.
4   With the whole class, ask students to make observations about the process of using the online dictionary. You could make notes of key points on the board. Which dictionary did they use? How useful was it? How easy was it to use? What sort of information did it give? Would they recommend it? Would they use it next time?

Multilingual contexts: see page 10

This activity can be used with both Type A and Type B classes. During the group discussion stage, it does not matter if the students refer to different bilingual dictionaries as they work to improve their drafts. In fact, the cross-checking of different bilingual dictionaries can make the activity even richer.

4.2 Using online dictionaries 2 (talking about news stories)

Outline	Students use online dictionaries to read two texts and to prepare short presentations on the topic of the texts. They also explore and discuss their use of online dictionaries.
Level	B1+
Time	Approximately 30 minutes (plus a few minutes to set up the activity in a previous lesson)
Preparation	None, but students will need online access out of class.

Procedure

1   Unless the classroom has online access, this activity will depend on students doing homework and will need to be set up in a previous lesson. Tell the students that their homework task is to find and choose a short news story (about 200 words is appropriate for a B1 learner) from a news website in their own language. This must be something that is international (i.e. not only of interest to people in their own country) and that they find interesting. It could be current affairs, or related to sport or entertainment. Their task will be to prepare a short, oral presentation, in English, about the news story for the next lesson.

2   Tell the students to follow the following steps.

   • Find an interesting news story in their own language. Cut and paste this story into a Word document.
   • Select a maximum of seven words from the story that they do not know how to express in English. Tell them to look up these words in an online dictionary (see the introduction to this chapter) and annotate their Word document. Tell them not to use an online translation tool.
   • Tell them to find a version of the same story on an English-language news website. You may need to give some suggestions of suitable sites, such as the following:
      BBC News: www.bbc.co.uk/news
      CNN: edition.cnn.com
      The Guardian (British newspaper): www.theguardian.com
      The New York Times (American newspaper): international.nytimes.com
   • In most cases, however, it should not be difficult to find an English version of the story simply by entering the key words (e.g. names) in a search engine and clicking the 'News' button on the toolbar.
   • Tell them to cut and paste this English version of the story into their Word document. Again, they should select a maximum of seven words from the story that they do not know how to express in their own language. Tell them to look up these words in an online dictionary and annotate their Word document.
   • They should now prepare their presentation. They should make notes (i.e. not write a full script or complete sentences) and it may be a good idea to point out that they will not be penalised for making mistakes. They should comment on any differences in the informational content of the two versions. At higher levels, they could also comment on any differences in style or the position taken by the writers of the different versions.

   It may be useful to write these steps on the board in note form.

3 Begin the next lesson by organising the class into groups (three or four students per group). In their groups, they should take it in turns to give their presentations. Students may refer to their notes and the original stories. These should not be formal presentations and other members of the group may ask questions about the story or ask for clarification of the language.

4 With the whole class, ask if anyone heard a particularly interesting story. Ask a few individual students to describe, briefly, the story they just heard.

5 Ask the class which dictionaries they used. Write these on the board. Ask students for evaluations of these dictionaries: How easy were they to use? Did they give too much or too little information? Which dictionaries were good enough for finding the meanings of the English words and which were better for finding ways to express in English the words from their own language? Conclude the activity by giving your own recommendations for online dictionaries.

Multilingual contexts: see page 10

This activity can be used with both Type A and Type B classes with no adaptation. The greater the number of own-language backgrounds in the class, the more the activity has potential for exploring intercultural issues.

4.3 Using online translation tools 1 (word lists)

Outline	Students revise vocabulary from a text they have previously studied. At the same time, they explore the limitations of online translation.
Level	All levels
Time	Approximately 10 minutes (for a list of around 7 words)
Preparation	Prepare a list of words or phrases (from a text that your students will study in class) that are important for your students to learn. Type this list of words and phrases into an online translation tool. Keep a note of your list of words/phrases and the translations that have been offered (some of which, of course, may be incorrect). In the example below (Figure 4.1), for French-speaking students, five of the nine translations are incorrect (marked *).

Procedure

1   After studying the text in class, write the list of words/phrases and their translations on the board. Tell the students that the translations come from an online translation tool: some are accurate, others are not. Ask the students to work in pairs and decide which of the translations are acceptable, and which are not. They may consult dictionaries, smartphone apps, or any other available resources (including online translation tools). See Activity 4.7: *Dictionary cross-checking*.

2   Conduct feedback with the whole class, referring students back to the text to justify their answers. Establish clearly which translations are accurate and which are not, and why.

Text

On Christmas Eve 1971, Juliana Koepcke, a seventeen-year-old German girl, left Lima by air with her mother. They were on their way to Pucallpa, another town in Peru, to spend Christmas with Juliana's father. Forty-five minutes later the plane broke up in a storm, and Juliana fell 3,000 metres, strapped in her seat. She was not killed when the seat hit the ground (perhaps because trees broke her fall), but she lay all night unconscious.

Word list and French translations provided by online translation tool

seventeen-year-old	*dix-sept ans*	strapped	*à court d'*
by air	*par avion*	in her seat	*dans son siège*
on their way to	*sur le chemin de*	hit the ground	*toucher le sol*
spend Christmas	*passer Noël*	lay	*poser*
broke up	*rompu*		

Figure 4.1: Adapted from Swan, M. & Walter, C. (1990) *The New Cambridge English Course Student 2,* Cambridge: Cambridge University Press, p. 26

Multilingual contexts: see page 10

This activity is not appropriate for Type A classes. In Type B classes, where the students share one language which the teacher cannot speak, the activity can be used if the teacher is prepared to accept being no more of an expert than the students: the teacher and the students explore the language together.

4.4 Using online translation tools 2 (texts)

Outline	Students hear or read a machine-translated text in their own language as preparation for reading a parallel text in English. Their attention is also drawn to the limitations of online translation tools.
Level	All levels (children over 14, in view of the level of cognitive maturity required, and adults)
Time	5 minutes
Preparation	Select a text which the students are going to read or to listen to in class. This could be the next text they are going to study in a coursebook, or something from an authentic source that is appropriate for the group. If the text is quite long, use only the first 100–150 words. Translate the text in an online tool, and keep a record of this translation, as in the example below (Figure 4.2).

Procedure

1   Before asking the class to read the selected text and do the accompanying exercises (if there are any in the coursebook), tell them that you have translated the text online into their language. Before they read the text in English, tell them that you are first going to read aloud the online translation.

2   Read the translation aloud to the class, making the most of your gestures and intonation to indicate where there are language errors (highlighted in Figure 4.2). You may also comment on the problems in the translation, and it's best to do this in a jokey way. If you prefer, you could project the translation onto the board and students read it silently and quickly.

3   Tell the class to read the English text and do any reading tasks that you wish to set.

Text machine-translated into French

Le lendemain matin, Juliana cherché morceaux de l'avion, et a appelé à sa mère. Personne ne répondit, et elle ne trouva rien, sauf un petit sac en plastique de bonbons. Juliana clavicule était cassée, un genou a été grièvement blessé et elle a eu de fortes réductions sur les bras et les jambes. Elle n'avait pas de chaussures, ses lunettes ont été brisées (si elle ne pouvait pas voir des serpents ou des araignées, par exemple), et elle ne portait qu'une robe très courte, qui a été déchirée.

English text

The next morning Juliana looked for pieces of the plane, and called for her mother. Nobody answered, and she found nothing except a small plastic bag of sweets. Juliana's collar bone was broken, one knee was badly hurt and she had deep cuts on her arms and legs. She had no shoes; her glasses were broken (so she could not see snakes or spiders, for example); and she was wearing only a very short dress, which was badly torn.

Figure 4.2: Adapted from Swan, M. & Walter, C. (1990) *The New Cambridge English Course Student 2,* Cambridge: Cambridge University Press, p. 26

Multilingual contexts: see page 10

This activity is not appropriate for Type A classes. In Type B classes, where the students share one language which the teacher cannot speak, the activity can be used if the projection option is used – or if the teacher is prepared to attempt to read the text aloud in the shared language! Clearly, the teacher cannot comment on the accuracy of the translation. The activity is still valuable without such comments.

4.5 Comparing online translation tools

Outline	Students compare two or more major online translation tools and evaluate their strengths and weaknesses.
Level	A2+
Time	Approximately 40 minutes
Preparation	Make copies of the handout for each student. Select a text (or an extract from a text) of an appropriate level (or slightly higher) for the class. Five or six lines of text are probably enough for the purposes of this activity. The text could be from a coursebook that you are using, or something authentic that is related to the topic of the lesson.
	Select a second short text in the students' own language. Find something online (e.g. from a news site) that is related to the English-language text. You will need to have both of these texts in a digital format, so you may need to type the coursebook text, if you are using that.
	If you have online access and a projector in the classroom, no further preparation is required. If you do not have these facilities, you will need to prepare translations in advance. Paste the English text into two or more different online translation tools and convert it into the students' own language. Save these translations so that you can project them onto the board in the classroom or distribute them as photocopies. Do the same with the text that is in the students' own language.

Free online translation varies in quality, the number of languages that are available and the amount of text that can be translated in one go. Some services are better with some languages than with others.

Procedure

1 Explain that you are going to look at some online translation tools. Tell the class to look first at the English text. They should read it quickly and say if they have problems understanding any of it. Resolve any problems.

2 Show the students two or more translated versions of this text. Indicate which translation tool has been used and give the students the relevant website address.

3 Draw their attention to one or two errors in the translations. Point out that, in many cases, errors are visible (to people using their own language) even if they do not understand the language which has been translated from.

4 Distribute the handout. Ask students to work in pairs. They should identify the errors in the translations and, using the handout as a guide, attempt to explain why these errors have occurred. With low levels, there is no reason why this discussion cannot be done in their own language.

5 Conduct feedback with the class and round off this stage of the lesson by asking the class which translation tool they think is the most reliable.

6 Tell the students to read the second text (in their own language) quickly. Then show them two or more translations of this text into English. Ask the students to work in pairs again and to identify errors in the English.

Do not give the class too long with this task. It is unlikely that they will be able to identify all the errors, but that is the point of the exercise! Conduct feedback with the whole class and identify any errors they have missed.

7 Conclude the activity by highlighting the disadvantages of online translation tools. You will probably want to make the following points.

- The level of accuracy is variable.
- Translating into one's own language gives us a reasonable grasp of the sense of the text, and we can often correct many problems ourselves.
- Translating into English is much more problematic because it is hard for us to identify what is accurate and what is inaccurate (unless our level of English is already very high and therefore we don't need the online translation!).

Multilingual contexts: see page 10
This activity cannot be used if the teacher does not share a language, other than English, with the students.

Online translation tools

There are a number of free online translation tools. Here are some of them:

Google Translate	translate.google.com
SDL FreeTranslation	www.freetranslation.com
Reverso	www.reverso.net
Bing Translator	www.bing.com/translator

These tools can help you to learn English, but you must be careful! Some of these tools will be more useful than others for your language. To use the tools well, you need to understand their limitations.

Online translation is not the same as a human translator. The machine translates literally: it does not 'think' about the meaning. Here are the most common language features that may not translate correctly.

1 Word order: online translation works better between languages that are similar to English, such as French, and not very well with languages such as Japanese with very different rules for word order.

2 Words with more than one meaning: the machine often does not select the correct meaning.

3 Object pronouns: the machine may not recognise what the pronoun refers to.

4 Articles (a, an, the).

5 Phrasal verbs and idiomatic expressions.

6 Complex sentences: for example, sentences with a relative clause.

7 Cultural references.

8 Style: for example, the formality of the language.

9 New or rare words.

10 Punctuation: for example, a comma can change the meaning of a sentence and the machine does not always recognise this.

Translating into your own language: be careful ... but you should be able to see many of the problems!

Translating into English: be extremely careful ... it may be difficult for you to see the problems!

4.6 Comparing dictionaries 1

Outline	Students explore different dictionaries in order to decide which kind is most appropriate for their needs.
Level	All levels
Time	Approximately 20 minutes
Preparation	Each group of students (three or four students per group) will need two or three different dictionaries. One of these should be a pocket bilingual dictionary, and one should be a larger bilingual dictionary. Each group could also look at a monolingual learner's dictionary. It is not necessary for each group to consult the same sets of dictionaries.

In order to have a sufficient number of dictionaries, ask students to bring one (or two) dictionaries into class on the day that you want to do this activity. It is worth checking to see which dictionaries they have in order to make sure that there is a variety of them.

If it is not possible to arrange for a sufficient number of dictionaries for each group, you could also select three different dictionaries yourself, and photocopy (or project) the three entries for the same headword (see Handout B for an example).

You will also need to project or to have photocopies of Handout A. For lower-level classes, you will need to translate this into the students' own language.

Procedure

1 Select a high-frequency English word that has more than one meaning. In the example (Handout B), the word *point* has been chosen. Other suitable words include: *business, dear, face, find, great, hand, kind, little, matter, mind, miss, money, present, room, side, sort* (see also Activities 7.5: *High-frequency English words*, and 7.6: *High-frequency English words (collocations)*). The word you choose could be something that the students have recently encountered or found problematic.
2 Organise the students into groups and ask them to look up this word in the different dictionaries they have brought. (Alternatively, distribute Handout B, if you are using this.) Project or distribute Handout A and tell the groups to follow the instructions.
3 Conduct feedback with the whole class. Focus on the last question in Handout A.

Multilingual contexts: see page 10

This activity is not appropriate for Type A classes. However, it can be used with Type B classes, even if the teacher does not share a language with the students.

Handout A

Comparing dictionariess

Your teacher will give you a word to look up in different dictionaries. Complete the questionnaire and compare the dictionaries. Then, answer the last question.

Does your dictionary ... ?	Yes (✓) or No (✗)	How useful is this feature? A = very useful B = quite useful C = not especially useful
give meanings that are easy to understand		
give the different meanings for a word in order of importance		
help you to select which meaning you need		
help you to avoid common mistakes or confusions with your own language		
show differences between British and American English		
show how formal or informal the word is		
give examples of the word in a phrase or a sentence		
give examples of other words that go together with this word (collocations)		
have any other useful features (if so, what)		

Which of these dictionaries will be most useful:

1) for reading English?

2) for writing in English?

Handout B

Diccionario Cambridge Klett Mini (2004), p. 478

point [pɔɪnt] **I.** *n* **1.** *(sharp end)* punta *f* **2.** GEO cabo *m* **3.** *(particular place)* punto *m* **4.** *(particular time)* momento *m*; **at this ~ in time** en este momento **5.** *(significant idea)* cuestión *f*; **to be beside the ~** no venir al caso; **to get to the ~** ir al grano **6.** *(in score)* punto *m*; **decimal ~** coma *f*, punto *m* decimal *AmL* **II.** *vi* señalar; *(indicate)* **III.** *vt* apuntar; **to ~ sth at sb** apuntar con algo a alguien
• **point out** *vt* indicar
point-blank *adv* a quemarropa; **to refuse** - negarse rotundamente
pointless ['pɔɪntləs] *adj* inútil
point of view <points of view> *n* punto *m* de vista

Diccionario Cambridge Klett Pocket (2002), p. 669

point [pɔɪnt] **I.** *n* **1.** *(sharp end)* punta *f* **2.** *(promontory)* cabo *m* **3.** *(particular place)* punto *m* **4.** *(particular time)* momento *m*; **boiling/ freezing ~** punto *m* de ebullición/ congelación; **starting ~** punto de partida; **to do sth up to a ~** hacer algo hasta cierto punto: **at this ~ in time** en este momento **5.** *(significant idea)* cuestión *f*; **to be beside the ~** no venir al caso; **to get to the ~** ir al grano; **to get the ~ (of sth)** entender (algo); **to make one's -** expresar su opinión; **to make a – of doing sth** procurar de hacer algo; **to miss the ~** no acptar lo relevante; **to take sb's ~** aceptar el argumento de alguin; **~ taken** de acuerdo; **that's just the -!** ¡eso es lo importante!; **what's the -?** ¿qué sentido tiene? **6.** *(in score)* punto *m;* **decimal ~** coma *f*, punto *m* decimal *AmL;* **to win on ~s** ganar por puntos **II.** *vi* señalar; *(indicate)* **III.** *vt* apuntar; **to ~ sth at sb** apuntar con algo a alguien; **to ~ a finger at sb** *a fig* señalar con el dedo a alguien; **to ~ sth toward sth** dirgir algo hacia algo; **to ~ sb toward sth** indicar a alguien el camino hacia algo
• **point out** *vt* indicar **to point sth out sb** (inform) advertir a alguien de algo
• **point-up** *vi form* destacar
point-blank *adv* a quemarropa; **to refuse** - negarse rotundamente
pointed ['pɔɪntɪd], *Am;* [ɪd] *adj* **1.** (implement, stick) puntiagudo **2.** *fig criticism)* mordaz; (question) directo
pointer ['pɔɪntəʳ *Am;* [ə] *n* puntero *m*; (of clock) aguja *f*
pointless ['pɔɪntləs] *adj* inútil
point of view <points of view> *n* punto *m* de vista

Diccionario Cambridge Compact (2008), p. 452

point¹ /pɔɪnt/ ▮ *n* [c] **1** ➾ punta: *Be careful with the point of the pin* - Ten cuidado con la punta del alfiler **2** *(en deportes)* ➾ punto ➾ tanto **3** ➾ momento: *Just at that point, Peter sneezed* - Justo en ese momento, Peter estornudó ▮ Se dice *at that point.* Incorrecto: *in that point* **4** *(en geometría)* ➾ punto **5** *(en matemáticas)* ➾ con ➾ coma **6** *(medida)* ➾ punto **7** ➾ lugar ➾ punto: *the starting point* - el punto de partida **8** *(calidad)* ➾ punto **9** *(en geografía)* ➾ promontorio **10** ➾ cuestión ➾ punto ▮ *n* [NO PL] **11** ➾ razón ➾ motivo: *What is the point of your visit?* - ¿Cuál es el motivo de tu vista? **12** ➾ sentido: *There is no point in waiting any longer* - No tiene sentido seguir esperando; *What's the point?* - ¿Qué sentido tiene? **13 on the ~ of** ➾ a punto de: *I was on the point of leaving* - Estuve a punto de irme **14 the ~** ➾ la cuestión principal **15 to be beside the ~** ➾ no tener nada que ver ➾ ser irrelevante **16 to the ~ - 1** ➾ conciso,sa: *Her article is short and to the point-* Su artículo es breve y conciso **2** ➾ al grano *col.: to get to the point* - ir al grano **17 up to a ~** ➾ en parte
☐ Véase tb: a **sore** (point/spot/subject); **boiling point; match point; moot point; power point; selling point; strong point; talking point; to be one's strong point; to miss** the point; **turning point; vantage point**
point² /pɔɪnt/ *v* (T, I) **1** ➾ señalar [con el dedo]: *I pointed to the cake I wanted* - Señalé el pastel que quería **2** ➾ apuntar: *to point a gun at sth* – apuntar con una pistola a alguien **3** ➾ mirar [hacia una dirección]: *This house points towards the south* - Esta casa mira hacia el sur **4** *(en una pared, en un muro)* ➾ repasar las juntas ➾ rejuntar
PHRASAL VERBS
• **to point sth/sb out** [M] **1** ➾ señalar: *The little boy pointed out a kite* – El niño señaló una cometa; ➾ in-

4.7 Dictionary cross-checking

Outline	Students practise dictionary cross-checking to improve their skills with bilingual (pocket) dictionaries.
Level	All levels
Time	10–15 minutes
Preparation	This activity should be used as part of the preparation for speaking or writing activities. Students will need access to bilingual pocket dictionaries or online dictionaries (e.g. of the kind that can be used with smartphones). You will need to remind students in a previous lesson to bring these into class.

Procedure

1   Before a speaking activity, give students time to brainstorm ideas for what they wish to say individually. The length of time needed for this will depend on the activity and on the level, but five minutes is usually enough. In order to generate more ideas, tell them that they can do this in their own language or a mixture of English and their own language (see Activity 2.3: *Own-language moments*). Tell them to take notes to help them to remember what they want to say.

2   Tell the students to get out their dictionaries and check how to say in English what they want to say. Explain that it is often a good idea to cross-check items that they look up in small dictionaries (i.e. look up the English translation of a word in their own language, and then check the translations into their own language of the English words they have found).

Give an example such as the following. A student checks the French word *carnaval* and the dictionary offers the English *carnival*. However, when you look up the English word *carnival*, you find two entries: *carnaval* and *fête foraine* (corresponding to the American use of *carnival* (and the British *funfair*).

Tell the students to do the same with any words in their own language that they have noted down and which they are not sure about. It is usually best to set a time limit of a few minutes in order to encourage students to prioritise their work (and not to look up every word).

In the example on page 63 (Figure 4.3), students have brainstormed and cross-checked ideas to talk about a festival they have been to.

Variations

This technique can be used equally effectively when students are (1) brainstorming ideas for writing, and (2) editing their writing.

Students can also be encouraged to check first in a bilingual dictionary and do the cross-checking in a monolingual learner's dictionary.

Note

The limitations of small bilingual dictionaries are obvious to language teachers, but less so to our students. Ideally, they would use larger dictionaries (i.e. Learner's dictionaries), but bilingual versions of these exist for only a small number of languages, and many students are reluctant to carry around heavier books of this kind. Bowing to 'force majeure', we can, at least, help our students use pocket dictionaries more critically.

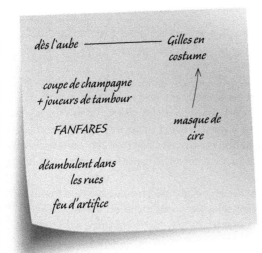

French–English search results

costume	suit, costume
coupe	cut, haircut, cup, goblet, glass
fanfare	brass band, fanfare
cire	wax, polish
déambuler	meander, walk around
feu d'artifice	firework, firework display, fireworks

Selected English–French search results (and notes)

suit	costume, tailleur
costume	costume

Knowing that the French word *costume* has two different meanings, the student should be able to work out that the English word *costume* (and not *suit*) is the word needed here.

cup	tasse, coupe
goblet	gobelet
glass	verre

It should be possible to eliminate immediately *cut* and *haircut*. Cross-checking should lead the student towards selecting *glass*, rather than *cup* or *goblet* (although both are possible).

brass band	fanfare
fanfare	fanfare

Cross-checking is more circular and less immediately helpful here, but a cross-check with the word *brass* (= *cuivre jaune*) will make things clear.

Figure 4.3: Student's brainstormed notes and translations

Multilingual contexts: see page 10

This activity can be used with both Type A and Type B classes with no adaptation.

4.8 Comparing dictionaries 2

Outline	Students translate sentences containing high-frequency words in order to compare different dictionaries and to practise dictionary skills.
Level	A2+
Time	Approximately 25 minutes
Preparation	Each group of students (three or four students per group) will need access to two or three different bilingual dictionaries. These can be print or digital dictionaries. It is not necessary for each group to consult the same sets of dictionaries. In order to have a sufficient number of dictionaries, ask students to bring one (or two) into class on the day that you want to do this activity. It is worth checking to see which dictionaries they have in order to make sure that there is a variety of them.

Select a high-frequency English word that has more than one meaning. In the example below, the word *ground* has been chosen. Other suitable words include: *business, dear, face, find, great, hand, kind, little, matter, mind, miss, money, present, room, side, sort* (see also Activities 7.5: *High-frequency English Words*, and 7.6: *High-frequency English Words (collocations)*). The word you choose could be something that the students have recently encountered or had problems with. Prepare a list of sentences that illustrate the different meanings of this word.

Procedure

1 Write the sentences that illustrate the target word on the board. Alternatively, you could dictate these sentences.
2 Organise the students into groups and tell them to translate the sentences into their own language. Encourage them to use the different dictionaries. They will find it useful to keep the dictionaries open at the page which shows the entry for the target word.
3 Conduct feedback with the whole class and agree on a translation for each of the sentences.
4 Put the students back into their groups again. Ask them to decide which dictionary they found most useful and to explain their reasons.
5 Conduct feedback again with the whole class.

Ground:

- My bag fell on the *ground*.
- Where's the nearest football *ground* to here?
- Many night animals have their homes below *ground*.
- Prepare the *ground* carefully before planting these flowers.
- You need *ground* beef to make spaghetti bolognese.
- We need to establish some *ground* rules.
- They live on the *ground* floor of the building.
- After last week's fall, share prices are gaining *ground* again.

Multilingual contexts: see page 10

This activity can be used with both Type A and Type B classes. With Type A classes, students work individually, rather than in groups.

4.9 Using word processor tools

Outline Students practise using word processing tools (bilingual dictionary and thesaurus) to edit their written work.

Level A2+

Time 40 minutes +

Preparation This activity, like Activity 4.1: *Using online dictionaries 1*, is intended to be used in the context of writing skills development. After students have brainstormed ideas for producing a particular piece of writing (e.g. a narrative, an email, a composition), and after they have shaped these ideas into a plan, encourage them to write a first draft very fast. They should feel free to include elements from their own language (words and phrases), to leave blanks, to use diagrams and annotations – anything that will help them get their ideas down quickly. You will need one student's piece of work, in digital format, to demonstrate.

The activity can be done in the classroom if students have access to computers, laptops or smartphones with word processing programmes such as Microsoft Word. Remember that online access is needed for the translation functions. If this is not possible, the teacher can prepare screenshot slides (to project in class) in which the various stages of using the word processor tools can be demonstrated. Students can then experiment themselves with computers outside and after the class.

It is not essential that every student has individual access: groups of three will work well. If the classroom is not wired, students can also be asked to do this work as a homework assignment.

Procedure

1 Demonstrate how to highlight a word, either in English or in the students' own language and how to check its translation. If they are translating from their own language into English, remind them to cross-check the word (see Activity 4.7: *Dictionary cross-checking*).

2 Demonstrate how to highlight a word, in English, and use the thesaurus function to find possible alternatives. The example on page 66 (Figure 4.4) uses the French word *indispensable*. Remind them that they will need to translate some of these English words into their own language.

3 Demonstrate how to highlight a whole phrase, in their own language, and translate it into English. Remind them that the translation isn't necessarily accurate!

4 Demonstrate how to run a spell check on an English-only draft of their work. Tell them that the grammar-check is usually of very limited value, but that the spell-check is a quick way of eliminating a few mistakes. Of course, some perfectly correct items will be highlighted in a spell-check, for example proper names which the dictionary does not recognise, but these are usually quite low in number and should be double-checked.

5 Organise the students into pairs or groups of three. Ask them to look at their rough drafts in turn. They work together, using all the resources at their disposal and their shared ideas to improve each draft. If the piece of work is about 150 words long, they will probably need about ten minutes per draft, but this could be longer, depending on level.

6 Individual students then work another five minutes on their own draft, before submitting it.

7 The teacher briefly comments on the work and uses a highlighter (either a highlighting pen, or a highlighting function on a digital document) to indicate where the student could usefully check something with translation or dictionary/thesaurus tools again. The work is returned to the student to write another draft.

8   With the whole class, ask students to make observations about the process of writing drafts in this way. You could make notes of key points on the board. Which tools did they use? How useful were they? How easy were they to use? What sort of information did they give? Would they recommend them? Would they use them next time?

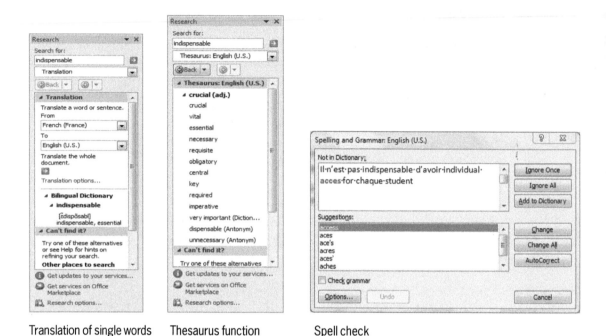

Translation of single words   Thesaurus function   Spell check

Figure 4.4: Word processing tools, used with permission from Microsoft.

Multilingual contexts: see page 10

This activity can be used with both Type A and Type B classes. With Type A classes, students work individually, rather than in groups, during Stage 5 (when they improve their drafts).

4.10 Using a search engine as a corpus check

Outline	Students practise using a search engine to check the accuracy of English phrases.
Level	B1+
Time	Approximately 15 minutes
Preparation	The students will need online access. If this is not possible in the classroom, the activity can be done as homework (see below).

Select a text in the students' own language and translate it into English using an online translation tool. Identify four or five problems with the translation, and cut and paste the problematic phrases into a document. Keep a note, too, of how these phrases were expressed in the original version. Add two or three phrases which are perfectly accurate. Jumble the order of the phrases up, so that the problematic phrases are not all together. You will need to be able to project this onto the board in the classroom. Alternatively, you could make photocopies of this document (in which case, the activity could be set as a homework task).

Instead of using English that has been generated by an online translation tool, you could collect samples of students' writing when you are correcting a batch of their written work. The kinds of errors that work best for this activity are word order and collocation problems.

Procedure

1   Ask the students to look at the list of phrases. Explain where the phrases come from (i.e. from an online translation or from the students' own work). Tell the students how many of the phrases are incorrect.

2   Explain that one way of checking whether a phrase (not more than about seven words) in English is acceptable or not is to enter it into a search engine. Demonstrate this with one correct and one incorrect phrase from the list. Point out that the phrase should be placed between inverted commas to ensure that the search engine searches for the complete phrase and not individual words within the phrase.

In the example on page 68, from a text translated from German, *I let myself be surprised* generates over 50,000 hits. Even though the first hit is a discussion about whether or not this phrase is acceptable or an over-literal translation (from German), the number of hits and the examples that follow indicate that the phrase could be acceptable. The second item on the list, *if something else is for me*, generates no hits at all, despite the fact that each word in the phrase is high frequency. This suggests that the phrase is unlikely to be acceptable. The precise number of hits will vary over time, but this still provides useful guidance.

3   Organise the class into pairs and tell them to go through the other items on the list in the same way.

4   Conduct feedback with the whole class, ensuring that everyone is clear about what is and is not acceptable. As you are doing this, make the following points.

- This kind of check is not fool-proof, but it can be a very useful way of seeing if something is probable or not.
- The technique works best with phrases that contain about five to eight words. If there are fewer words than this, almost everything will generate a substantial number of hits.
- It is a good idea to look closely at the first four or five hits. It is not normally necessary to open the link. The context that is given on the search results page is usually enough to see how the phrase will fit into a longer stretch of language.

- Students can use this technique when they have used online translation or when they are checking their own writing.

Example

- *I let myself be surprised* (50, 400 hits)
- *if something else is for me* (0 hits)
- *presented after his number one hit* (0 hits)
- *sad to have to leave the show* (7 hits)
- *the casting format show* (0 hits)
- *the written especially for her song* (4 hits)
- *wants to make a musical education* (0 hits)

Multilingual contexts: see page 10

This activity can be used with both Type A and Type B classes. The technique can be demonstrated using examples of language from the students' own work.

4.11 Word cards

Outline	Students learn vocabulary with bilingual word cards.
Level	All levels
Time	Variable
Preparation	You will need a set of blank white cards, ideally of filing-card size, but you can use pieces of paper that have been cut up. If possible, supply the students with five sheets of A4 paper/card each. If not, ask them to bring this material into class. The paper/card can be cut up into 40 smaller rectangles, and this is enough to start with.

Procedure

1 Introduce the idea of word cards and explain their use (see *Note* on page 70). Show the students some examples of word cards, with the English word/phrase/chunk on one side, and a translation on the other.

2 Tell the students to look back in their notes, or in the book they are using, and to identify words that they have trouble remembering or have already forgotten. If they are using a coursebook, there may be a word list corresponding to units of the book. Students could also go through such lists to identify 'problem words'.

3 Tell the students to write the 'problem words' they have found on to the cards. Using dictionaries, if necessary, they write the translations on the other side. Encourage the students to include other useful information, such as frequency indicator (if included in the dictionary entry), part of speech, common collocations, pronunciation, cognates, antonyms, etc.

4 Once the students have a pack (of more than ten cards), show them how they should use the cards as in Figure 4.5 below.

- Go through the cards, one at a time, looking at the English side first. Can you remember what the word means? If not, check the other side of the card, and then put the card in the middle of the pack. If yes, check you are right, and then put the card at the back of the pack.

- Go through the pack once or twice, put it away, but return to it about 30 minutes later. Do it again later that day, the next day, after a few days, and so on.

- Shuffle the pack from time to time.

- After a few days, take out the words that you are sure you have no problems with. Add more cards to the pack.

- Use the word cards that you discard as a second pack. This time, go through them looking at the translation into L1 first. Can you remember the English?

Figure 4.5: Adapted from Nation, I.S.P. (2008) *Teaching Vocabulary: Strategies and Techniques*, Boston: Heinle Cengage, p. 106

5 Allocate short periods of class time, from time to time, for students to test each other with their word cards.

Variation

Students lucky enough to have smartphones can now download apps which are basically digitalised bilingual word cards. A small set of pre-prepared cards is usually supplied, but users can edit and make their own cards very quickly and easily. The British Council's MyWordBook can be found at: learnenglish. britishcouncil.org/en/mobile-learning. Other popular wordcard/flashcard programmes are Byki (www.byki.com) and Anki (ankisrs.net).

Note

Nation (2008) suggests that a good way to learn a lot of words quickly is to use word cards, or something similar. However, in order to become part of our active repertory, we also need opportunities to try using these words, orally, for preference.

Multilingual contexts: see page 10

This activity can be used with both Type A and Type B classes.

4.12 Using monolingual tools: making a glossary

Outline	Students translate rubrics from a monolingual resource (such as a grammar book) in order (1) to study basic classroom metalanguage in English, and (2) to make it easier to use this resource in the future.
Level	A2–B1
Time	Variable (depending on level and the number of items to be translated)
Preparation	Prepare a list of phrases (e.g. from a grammar book) that the students will need to understand in order to use the material. It would be useful to tabulate the phrases if possible (as in Figure 4.6 below) so as to show how the expressions are built up, but this is not strictly necessary.

Procedure

1 Write the phrases on the board (or distribute them as a handout).
2 Organise the students into pairs or small groups. Their task is to translate anything that they do not understand into their own language. They can use any resources at their disposal to do this.
3 Conduct feedback with the whole class. Resolve any queries. Students should ensure that they can, in future, easily access their translated phrase list (i.e. whenever they are working from the resource that has been focused on in this way).

Correct	the sentences		where necessary.		
Complete	the conversations (them)		with	the following verbs	in the correct form.
Make Write	sentences (the / your) questions		using	the words in brackets	as (shown) in the example (s).

Use	your own ideas the words in brackets the verb	to	complete make	(the) sentences. (the) questions.
Put	the words in brackets the verbs	into the correct form.		

Sometimes you	need must use	the	negative. continuous/simple form.

Are the	underlined verbs	right or wrong? correct or incorrect?

Figure 4.6: Glossary of classroom metalanguage

Note
This activity could also be set as a homework task.

Multilingual contexts: see page 10

This activity can be used with Type A classes if students work individually. With Type B classes, students can be organised into language groups.

4.13 Dual language resources exchange

Outline	Students explore dual-language resources for learning English outside the classroom and share their ideas in short class presentations.
Level	All levels
Time	Approximately 20 minutes to set up the activity; then approximately eight minutes per presentation. Finally, approximately another 25 minutes in a later lesson.
Preparation	Make a sufficient number of photocopies of the handout for each student. It will also be helpful if you have identified, in advance, your own personal preferences for out-of-class resources.

Procedure

1 Ask the class if they have any ideas for improving their English outside the classroom (in addition to homework, of course!). It may be a good idea to begin by giving a few ideas of useful materials yourself. You may get some initial ideas from the list below. Write each idea in note form on the board and discuss each one briefly. When the class has run out of ideas, add some more of your own.

2 Explain that you want each student in the class to research one idea and to present their research to the rest of the class. These presentations will take place over a number of lessons: one or two presentations per lesson will be enough. Allocate, through a combination of volunteering and nomination, one resource idea to each student. Point out that the presentations should be done in English (except for very low-level classes, for which you will also need to translate the handout).

3 Distribute the handout. Check to ensure that everyone understands the task. Arrange a timetable for the first four or five presentations.

4 Begin subsequent lessons with one or two presentations. Allow a few minutes afterwards for questions. Attach the poster presentations to the walls of the classroom. If this is not possible, store them somewhere where they can be consulted at a later date.

5 In a lesson after all the presentations have been given, give the students about ten minutes to look at the posters again. Ask if anyone in the class has experimented with one or more of these resources and if they agree with the evaluation of the student who originally presented it.

6 Organise the students into groups and ask them to select the best five resources and put them in order of usefulness. With the whole class, bring the ideas of the different groups together and draw up a collective 'Top Five' list.

Note

It would be extremely useful to share the work that has been done with other classes.

Suggestions for materials for improving English outside the classroom

There is an enormous amount of material for English language learners, and it is not really possible to give more than a few specific suggestions. The list on page 73 focuses on materials that use other languages, but there is, of course, no reason to restrict your students to these. If they do not feel that they need the support of their own language, the possibilities are almost endless.

- Supplementary learning aids (books, DVDs, software) on sale in major bookshops around the world. These include help with grammar, vocabulary, pronunciation and skills work. A huge range of such commercial material is produced by both international and local publishers, and much of it is dual-language. The quickest way to find the best shop nearest to you is to check out the local distributors of the major international publishers. These can be found through the publishers' websites.
- Language learning apps (some of these are free) for iTunes and Android.
- Online English language learning materials – much of this is free, but of variable quality.
- Games for learning English (to find ideas, type 'games for learning English', in either English or the students' language, into a search engine).
- A wealth of material and ideas at the British Council's 'Learn English' website; there are versions of this site for French, Chinese and Arabic-speaking learners, as well as a version in English only (learnenglish.britishcouncil.org/en).
- A wealth of material and ideas at the 'Student Zones' of the major ELT publishers (see, for example, www.cambridge.org/gb/elt/students).
- Online conversation exchange sites such as www.mylanguageexchange.com or www.language-exchanges.org.
- Dual language books, magazines and comics (to find ideas, type 'dual language books comics magazines', in either English or the students' language, into a search engine).
- Magazines for learning English (to find ideas, type 'magazines for learning English', in either English or the students' own language, into a search engine).
- Websites for streamed English-language movies and TV series with subtitles.
- Websites for music videos with subtitles and/or translations.
- Websites for song lyrics with translations.

Multilingual contexts: see page 10
There is a little point in students giving presentations to the rest of the class about resources which are only relevant to learners of their own language background (if no one else in the class has the same background). However, many resources use only English and others are available in multiple language versions. With heterogeneous classes, teachers will probably want to negotiate the choice of resource with individual students or to allocate particular resources to particular students.

Resources for improving your English outside the classroom

You are going to prepare a presentation about one resource that can be used for improving English outside the classroom. This resource can be a book, a magazine, a newspaper, a website, a CD-Rom or DVD. You need to do two things:

- Prepare a short presentation (about five minutes) that you will give to the class in English.

- Prepare a poster version of your presentation. This will be displayed on the walls of the classroom.

Use the questions below to guide you in your presentation.

1 Where can you find your resource?

2 Can you describe the resource in a couple of sentences?

3 How much does it cost, or is it free?

4 In what ways can this resource help with your English?

5 Can you give two or three specific examples of things that you found interesting or useful with this resource?

6 How often have you used this resource, and what exactly did you do with it?

7 What did you like most and what did you like least about this resource?

8 Do you recommend this resource to other people? Why / Why not?

9 If the resource costs money, is it worth it?

10 Can you make any photocopies or print screenshots to illustrate the resource?

5 Reverse translation

What is reverse translation?

Reverse translation (also known as 'back translation') has been around for a long time, at least as far back as the 16th century when the Spanish humanist, Juan Luis Vives, and the English educationalist and scholar, Roger Ascham, recommended the technique.

It is not complicated: students are given a text to translate from one language to another; later, they translate it back again (without, of course, referring to the original). For example, a text is first translated out of English, into the students' own language, and the students then translate it back into English.

The point of reverse translation is not to reproduce the original text word-for-word. A final translated *product* may or may not be helpful. It will be of less significance than the process of getting there, a process through which a language may be learned. This process is likely to have richer learning potential if the work is collaborative. Through the process of working to and fro between languages, learners are presented with multiple opportunities to notice features of language and to experiment with using them. In fact, as one methodologist puts it, it 'forces noticing in a way that nothing else does' (Dellar, 2012). It can also draw attention to the cross-cultural nature of translation; it develops learners' critical use of online technology; and it can be fun. The case for adding reverse translation to any teacher's basic toolkit is a compelling one.

Figure 5.1: Frontispiece of *The Scholemaster* (Ascham, 1570)

Many variations on the basic idea are possible. Reverse translation can take as its starting point examples of language that have been chosen or scripted to focus on particular points of grammar or vocabulary (see for example Activities 5.5: *Model texts*, and 5.6: *Grammar or vocabulary revision with reverse translation*). It can also work with texts that have no focus on discrete language items, and also with texts that the learners have generated themselves. This chapter suggests only a relatively small number of options. It is easy to find others.

Which direction to go in?

The early proponents of reverse translation, Vives and Ascham, disagreed about the directions for these translations. Vives thought that learners should begin with a text in their own language, which they should translate into Latin, and then translate back into their own language. Ascham thought they should begin with a Latin text (Benson, 2000, pp. 40–1). These days, it probably makes most sense to begin with a text in the target language (i.e. English), the learners then translate it into their own language (assuming that they have sufficient own-language skills), and subsequently back into English. Translation into the target language is generally harder than translation into your own language because it 'presupposes a knowledge of the language into which one is to translate, and this is precisely the knowledge the L2 learner lacks' (Stern, 1992, p. 296). For learners below CEFR level B2, translating first into their own language is likely to be a more useful strategy. Higher-level learners, such as philology students following a course in translation, will benefit from working in both directions.

References

Ascham, R. (1570) *The Scholemaster*, London: John Daye. Available online at: http://www. gutenberg.org/ebooks/1844. [Last accessed 01 July 2013]

Benson, M. J. (2000) 'The secret life of grammar-translation' in Trappes-Lomax, H. (ed.) *Change and Continuity in Applied Linguistics*. BAAL / Multilingual Matters: Clevedon, England, pp. 40–1.

Dellar, H. (2012) 'In praise of non-native-speaker teachers part 4: Translation' Available online at http://hughdellar.wordpress.com/2012/06/18/in-praise-of-non-native-speaker-teachers-part-four-translation/. [Last accessed 01 July 2013]

Stern, H.H. (1992) (Allen, P. & Harley, B., eds.) *Issues and Options in Language Teaching*, Oxford: Oxford University Press.

5.1 Broken telephone reverse translation

Outline	A warmer activity in which students pass a spoken sentence around the class, translating it each time it is passed on.
Level	All levels
Time	5–10 minutes
Preparation	Select one or more sentences to be passed around the class. With a small group (up to ten students) one sentence will be enough; with larger classes, more sentences will be needed. Here are some ideas for the sorts of sentences you might select:

- the first sentence of a text that the students are going to read or listen to later in the lesson
- an interesting sentence from a text that the students have previously read
- a sentence which contains an item of vocabulary or grammar, or a feature of pronunciation, which the teacher will subsequently focus on
- a sentence generated by the first students themselves (in response to a question, put by the teacher, which is related to the theme of the lesson, e.g. *Describe, in a few words, someone you know who is not very honest.*)
- an interesting sentence from the news, a couple of lines from a pop lyric, an interesting quote, etc.

Procedure

1 Whisper a sentence in English to one student, who must translate it into their own language before passing it on, in translation and whispers, to the person sitting next to them. This person must translate it back into English, and whisper that to the next person. He or she will translate it back into their own language and pass it on, etc.

2 With larger classes, you can start a number of different sentences in different parts of the classroom. Make sure everyone is clear about who they should pass their sentence on to.

3 Stop the activity when the last student has been reached or when the broken telephone completely breaks down! Ask one of the last students to hear the sentence to repeat what they heard, in English. It is very unlikely that this will be the same as the sentence(s) that began the activity. Ask intermediary students what their sentences were and identify where, how and why the sentence got changed. Deal with any language issues (e.g. grammar) that arise.

Multilingual contexts: see page 10

This activity cannot be used in Type A classes. It can be used in Type B classes if there is a language which all the students share, even if the teacher does not speak this language.

5.2 Fold-over reverse translations

Outline	A warmer activity in which students pass a written sentence or short text around the class, translating it each time it is passed on.
Level	All levels
Time	Approximately 15 minutes
Preparation	You need to select at least two sentences or short texts to be passed around the class. With a small group (up to ten students) two sentences or texts will be enough; with larger classes, more sentences will be needed. For ideas for the sorts of sentences you might select, see Activity 5.1: *Broken telephone reverse translation*. The sentences should be written at the top of a sheet of A4 (or similar size) paper.

Procedure

1 Students work in pairs or small groups. Either, they are given the English text which they must translate into their own language, or they write a short text which they will then pass on for translation. They should leave a small space after the English text, and then write a version of this text in their own language. They should fold the top of the page backwards so that the English text cannot be seen, and only their translation is visible.

2 The turned-over pages are passed on to the next pair or group, whose task is to translate the text in front of them into English (without, of course, looking at the English text that has been hidden). When finished, they turn over the page once again, leaving only their own text visible, and pass it onto the next pair or group.

3 Continue in this way until you want the students to stop. Four or five changes are usually enough. Allow some time for discussion of the content of the text. Then, tell the pairs or groups to open their sheets of paper. Students will almost certainly have questions: what problems did they have? What did they find hard to translate? Which translations were acceptable? Why were some better than others?

The example on page 79 (Figure 5.2) comes from Jane Austen's *Pride and Prejudice* and is one of the most famous opening sentences in English novels.

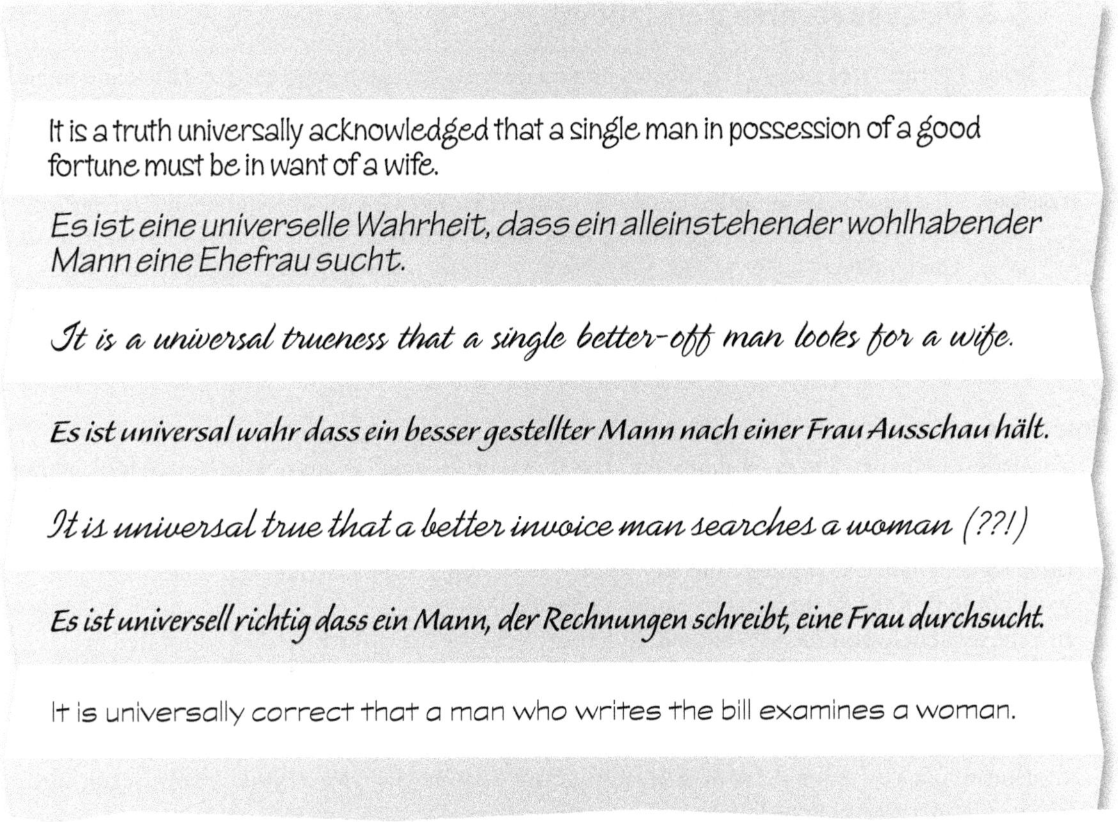

It is a truth universally acknowledged that a single man in possession of a good fortune must be in want of a wife.

Es ist eine universelle Wahrheit, dass ein alleinstehender wohlhabender Mann eine Ehefrau sucht.

It is a universal trueness that a single better-off man looks for a wife.

Es ist universal wahr dass ein besser gestellter Mann nach einer Frau Ausschau hält.

It is universal true that a better invoice man searches a woman (??!)

Es ist universell richtig dass ein Mann, der Rechnungen schreibt, eine Frau durchsucht.

It is universally correct that a man who writes the bill examines a woman.

Figure 5.2: Reverse translation of opening sentence from Jane Austen's *Pride and Prejudice*

Multilingual contexts: see page 10

This activity cannot be used in Type A classes. It can be used in Type B classes if there is a language which all the students share, even if the teacher does not speak this language.

5.3 Delayed reverse translations

Outline	Learners translate an English text into their own language. They translate it back into English in a subsequent lesson, and then compare their version with the original.
Level	All levels
Time	Variable, depending on length of text and level
Preparation	This activity is intended to be used in the latter part of a lesson where students have earlier read a text (e.g. for reading practice or because it contextualised a particular language item). This text might be from their coursebook, but it could also be something more authentic.
	Decide how much of the text you will ask the students to translate. For lower-level (A1 and A2) students, 40–80 words will be enough. For B1 and B2 students, 90–120 words will be enough.

Procedure

1   Towards the end of a lesson, organise the class into pairs or small groups. Ask them to look at the text or part of a text, and write a translation of it in their own language on a sheet of paper. This is collaborative work and you will need to decide if you wish to allow students to use dictionaries or other tools. Thank the students and collect their work when they have finished. If necessary, this work could be finished for homework and collected later.

2   In a subsequent lesson, ensure that the students cannot see the text which they translated in a previous lesson. Distribute the translated texts to the students who wrote them, and ask them to translate these back into English. Students will probably have queries and some will be very tempted to look at the original text. Don't answer the queries at this stage, but encourage the students to put a question mark in their translations (into English) for anything they are not sure about. Again, this is collaborative work.

3   When the students have gone as far as they can with their translations, tell them to look at the original text and to compare their version with it. Deal with any queries that arise.

Variations

1   Instead of using a paragraph for translation, you could also select extracts from a longer text: these might be key sentences, useful phrases or chunks of language which contain elements of grammar that you want to highlight. Remember to keep the task manageable: too much text to translate may be demotivating.

2   In the subsequent lesson, organise the class into groups of four. Instead of distributing the translated texts to the students who wrote them, distribute any two translations to each group. Using both of these texts, the group's task is to translate back into English. When they have completed this, they can compare their work with the original. They can also evaluate the two translations they worked from.

3   Instead of all the students working on the same text, select two different texts. These might be parts of a longer text which the students have read. Organise the class into pairs, and give each pair one of the texts to translate. When they have done this, reorganise the class into new pairs, where each member of the pair has translated a different text. The students work together on both translations to translate back, orally, into English, without consulting the original. Finally, they compare their work with the originals, noting any difficulties they had.

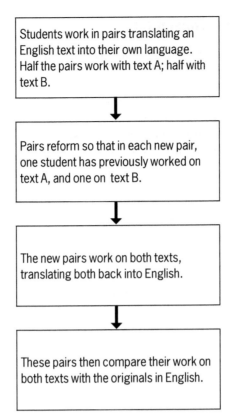

Students work in pairs translating an English text into their own language. Half the pairs work with text A; half with text B.

↓

Pairs reform so that in each new pair, one student has previously worked on text A, and one on text B.

↓

The new pairs work on both texts, translating both back into English.

↓

These pairs then compare their work on both texts with the originals in English.

Multilingual contexts: see page 10

This activity can be used with both Type A and Type B classes. In Type A classes, students will have to work individually when they are translating the text into their own language.

5.4 Gapped reverse translation

Outline	Learners reconstruct an English text with a gapped frame, using a translation of it in their own language.
Level	A2+
Time	Approximately 15 minutes, depending on length of text and level
Preparation	Select an English text of about 100 words. Count the number of words in each sentence. Translate this text into the students' own language. Make photocopies of this translation (one copy for every three students is enough).

Procedure

1 Hand out the translations. Write on the board (or project) a gapped frame for the text, using one write-on line for every word. Begin each new sentence on a new line. Write out in full any words that you think will be unknown and include punctuation marks, as in the example below (Figure 5.3).

_____ Babel Fish _____ _____ _____ _____ Douglas Adams _____ _____ _____ *The Hitchhiker's Guide to the*

Galaxy.

_____ _____ _____ _____ Babel Fish _____ _____ _____, _____ _____ _____ _____ _____ _____

_____ _____ _____ _____ .

_____ _____ _____ _____, _____ _____ _____ _____ _____.

_____ _____ _____ _____ _____ _____ _____ _____ _____ _____.

_____, _____ _____ _____ _____ _____ intergalactic _____ _____ _____ _____ _____ _____ _____ _____

_____ _____ _____ _____ .

Text

The Babel Fish was an idea of Douglas Adams in his novel *The Hitchhiker's Guide to the*

Galaxy.

When people put a Babel Fish in their ear, they could immediately understand everything that

people said to them.

At the same time, other people could understand them.

There were no more barriers to communication between different cultures.

Unfortunately, this technology led to more intergalactic wars in the universe than anything else since

the beginning of time.

Figure 5.3: Adapted from Adams, D. (1979) *The Hitchhiker's Guide to the Galaxy*, London: Pan

2   Organise the class into groups. Each group takes it in turn to call out one word that will be needed in the English text. If the word is indeed needed in the text, write it in the appropriate gap(s) on the board. Very high-frequency words (e.g. *the, is, of*) will, of course, occur more than once in the text.
3   Continue in this way until the text has been reconstructed. Some teachers turn this activity into a game and award points for correctly nominated words.

Multilingual contexts: see page 10

This activity can be done with both Type A and Type B classes if the students do the translation into their own language themselves. Once this has been completed, take back the English text and allow a few days to pass (as in Activity 5.3: *Delayed reverse translation*) before doing the activity.

5.5 Model texts

Outline	Students study a model text for an examination written task.
Level	B1+
Time	45 minutes (depending on text length)
Preparation	Find or write a model answer for an examination writing task. Translate this into the students' own language. You can find model answers to writing tasks for Cambridge English Language Assessment exams (e.g. FCE, CAE) in many coursebooks that prepare students for these exams, as well as dedicated websites.

Procedure

1 Draw students' attention to the task (in the example using German translation on page 85 (Figure 5.4) it is replying to a job advertisement), identify the written genre that is required, and hand out the model answer in English.
2 Draw students' attention to the organisation of ideas and paragraphs in the model.
3 Draw students' attention to useful phrases in the model. In the example below, these would include *I am writing in response to your ...*, *I am currently working as ...*, *I am interested in the position ...*, *I have included a copy of ...*, etc.
4 Take away the English version of the model and hand out the translation. In pairs or small groups, students must translate this into English.
5 When the students have finished, or when they have got as far as they can, let them see the original again. They should look for differences between the original and their version. For each version, they should decide (a) if their version was acceptable (b) which version was better.

Notes

Studying a text in this way can help learners to memorise chunks of it. In many exams, it is useful to have sets of useful phrases for particular written genres stored in the memory.

I would like to thank Roger Marshall for this idea.

Dear Sir or Madam,

I am writing in response to your advertisement in *The Daily News* on January 23rd for vacancies on your summer cruises. I am currently working as a part-time receptionist in a tourist complex in the north of Italy. I am interested in the position you are offering as it would enable me to extend my experience in the holiday industry.

I have worked as a waitress, chef's assistant and receptionist in the Italian Dolomites and on the Adriatic coast over the last two and a half years, and have enjoyed the work atmosphere as well as the chance to meet new people. I would be very interested in working for your organisation, as it would give me an opportunity to widen my horizons, both personally and professionally.

I have included a copy of my CV and the contact details for two referees. Thank you for your time and consideration.

Yours faithfully,

Angela Roth

 -

Sehr geehrte Damen und Herren,

Ich schreibe Ihnen bezüglich Ihrer Anzeige in *The Daily News* vom 23. Januar 2012 das Stellenangebot für Ihre Sommer-Kreuzfahrten betreffend.

Im Moment arbeite ich halbtags als Rezeptionistin in einem Touristenzentrum im Norden Italiens. Die Stelle, die Sie ausschreiben, interessiert mich deswegen besonders, weil sie mir mehr Einblick in die Tourismusbranche ermöglichen würde.

Ich habe bereits Erfahrungen als Kellnerin und Beiköchin gesammelt sowie die letzten zwei Jahre als Rezeptionistin wie bereits erwähnt in den Italienischen Dolomiten und an der Adriaküste. Gefallen hat mir dabei vor allem die Arbeitsstimmung und die Gelegenheit Leute kennen zu lernen. Ich wäre nun sehr interessiert für Ihre Organisation zu arbeiten, um meinen Erfahrungshorizont erweitern zu können, sowohl in persönlicher als auch professioneller Hinsicht.

Eine Kopie meines Lebenslaufes finden Sie anbei sowie die Kontaktdaten zweier Gutachter.

Ich danke Ihnen für Ihre Zeit, freue mich auf Ihre Antwort und verbleibe

mit freundlichen Grüßen

Angela Roth

Figure 5.4: Model text with translation

Multilingual contexts: see page 10

As in Activity 5.4: *Gapped reverse translation*, this activity can be done with both Type A and Type B classes if the students do the translation into their own language themselves. Once this has been completed, take back the English text and allow a few days to pass before doing the activity.

5.6 Grammar or vocabulary revision with reverse translation

Outline	The teacher dictates sentences (with a grammar or vocabulary focus) which the students immediately translate into their own language. They then translate these back into English.
Level	All levels
Time	15 minutes
Preparation	None, but the activity is a follow-up to any grammar or vocabulary exercise (e.g. a gap-fill or transformation exercise in a coursebook). The exercise should contain between six and eight sentences.

Procedure

1 After the students have completed the coursebook exercise, conduct feedback with the whole class.
2 Tell the students to close their books and take out a sheet of paper. Tell them that you are going to dictate some sentences. They *must not* write them down in English. They must immediately translate them into their own language and write down these sentences.
3 Dictate the sentences, allowing the students sufficient time to write their translated versions. Monitor their work.
4 The students work in pairs. Tell the students to work with their partner. They can consult both sets of translated sentences, and must translate them back into English, without consulting their coursebook.
5 Conclude the activity by allowing the students to look at the original sentences in the coursebook and by answering any questions that the students ask, or by discussing anything interesting that you have noticed while monitoring.

Note

Scott Thornbury suggests that this activity lends itself well to groups of sentences that contain contrasting verb patterns, e.g. gerunds and infinitives or dependent prepositions (Thornbury, S. (2006) *Grammar*, Oxford: Oxford University Press).

Variation

Other variations of this activity can be found in Chapter 7.

Multilingual contexts: see page 10

This activity can be used with both Type A and Type B classes with no modification.

5.7 Reverse translating using an online translation tool

Outline	Students use reverse translation to explore texts using an online translation tool.
Level	B1+
Time	30–45 minutes
Preparation	Select a text (Text A) that you want the students to work on. This should be an authentic text of intrinsic interest and be of an appropriate level. As an introduction to this kind of task, you could use the text on page 88 (*How does it work?*) with a B2 class. Translate the text into the students' own language. Copy and paste your translation of the text (Text B) into the translation program and convert into English. Save this document (Text C). Highlight any words/phrases in this translation that are incomprehensible or incorrect. The example on page 88 (Figure 5.5) shows a translation from Dutch with the errors highlighted.

Procedure

1 Generate interest in the topic of the text. If you use the text on page 88, you could ask if anyone has used online translation tools. If so, ask what for, how often, why, and what they think of them.
2 Show the students Text C and explain that this is a translation of a text that was originally written in their own language. Point out that it contains errors (highlighted in the text).
3 The class works in pairs or small groups. Tell the students to translate the text back into their own language. They should do this orally, and they should ignore the highlighted words for the moment.
4 Once the students have completed their oral translations, show them Text B, which is written in their own language. They should now look at the highlighted words and improve the translation into English.
5 Students can then compare their answers with Text A, the original in English.
6 Wrap up the activity by asking students how they feel about using online translation programs now. What tips would they give to other users?

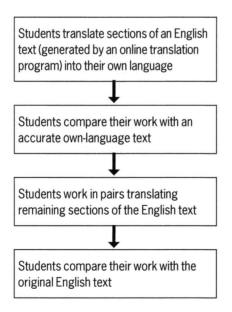

Students translate sections of an English text (generated by an online translation program) into their own language

↓

Students compare their work with an accurate own-language text

↓

Students work in pairs translating remaining sections of the English text

↓

Students compare their work with the original English text

TEXT A

How does Google Translate work?

When Google Translate generates a translation, it looks for patterns in hundreds of millions of documents to help decide on the best translation for you. By detecting patterns in documents that have already been translated by human translators, Google Translate can make intelligent guesses as to what an appropriate translation should be. This process of seeking patterns in large amounts of text is called "statistical machine translation". Since the translations are generated by machines, not all translation will be perfect. The more human-translated documents that Google Translate can analyse in a specific language, the better the translation quality will be. This is why translation accuracy will sometimes vary across languages.

translate.google.com/about

TEXT B

Hoe werkt Google Translate?

Wanneer een vertaling wordt gegenereerd met Google Translate, wordt gezocht naar patronen in honderden miljoenen documenten om te bepalen wat de beste vertaling voor u is. Door patronen te detecteren in documenten die al zijn vertaald door menselijke vertalers, kan Google Vertalen intelligente gissingen doen met betrekking tot wat een passende vertaling moet zijn. Het zoeken van patronen in grote hoeveelheden tekst wordt 'statistische machinevertaling' genoemd. Aangezien de vertalingen worden gegenereerd door computers, zijn niet alle vertalingen perfect. Hoe meer door mensen vertaalde documenten Google Vertalen kan analyseren in een bepaalde taal, hoe beter de kwaliteit van de vertaling wordt. Daarom verschilt de nauwkeurigheid van de vertaling soms per taal.

TEXT C

What is Google Translate?

If a translation is generated using Google Translate, searching for patterns in hundreds of millions of documents to determine what the best translation for you. By detecting patterns in documents already translated by human translators, Google Translate make intelligent guesses as to what should be an appropriate translation. Finding patterns in large amounts of text is called 'statistical machine translation' called. Since the translations are generated by computers, not all translations are perfect. The more people translated by Google Translate can analyze documents in a particular language, the better the quality of the translation. Therefore, the accuracy of translation is different times for each language.

Figure 5.5: Reverse translation from Google Translate. Google and the Google logo are registered trademarks of Google Inc., used with permission.

Variation

This technique is a useful way of revisiting texts that have already been studied in class. These could be, for example, from a coursebook. It is often more rewarding to return to material that has already been studied in depth in class than to move on to something completely new. Dialogues, news articles and encyclopaedia extracts can also be exploited in this way.

Multilingual contexts: see page 10

This activity is not suitable for Type A classes. It can, however, be used with Type B classes where there is one shared language, even if the teacher does not speak this language.

5.8 Reverse translating English as a Lingua Franca

Outline	Students explore bad translations between English and their own language.
Level	A2+ (depending on the materials used)
Time	Variable (depending on quantity and length of material)
Preparation	Find examples of bad translations into English from the students' own language. Besides the English that is found in the commercial streets of almost every town in the world (see also Activity 7.8: *Street English*), examples can usually be quickly found by entering "bad translations English + (*name of students' own language*)" into a search engine, either written in English or in the other language. You may also find examples of bad translations from English into the students' language, and these can be exploited too. Frequent sources for such translations include: labels on packaging, instructions on commercial products, notices (e.g. in hotels, at airports, stations, tourist offices), shop windows, advertising slogans, T-shirts, product names, menus, film subtitles. Some of the translations will be humorous: so much the better!

Procedure

1 Show the students the material you have found. If necessary, point out the error(s) in translation.
2 Using dictionaries and other resources, students work in pairs to deduce the original text in their own language, and then suggest an alternative translation in English.
3 Conduct feedback with the whole class.

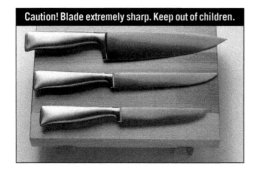

Variations

Alternative sources of bad translations which can be used in this way include: machine-translated text and the students' own work!

Note

A very entertaining source of mistranslations is Pedro Carolino's *English as she is spoke* (1883), a facsimile of which is available online at www.s4ulanguages.com/english-as-she-is-spoke.html. The dialogue on page 91 (Figure 5.6) is a good example. Carolino's book was intended for speakers of Portuguese, but Carolino himself probably could not speak English.

To Inform One'self of a Person

How is that gentilman who you did speak by and by?

Is a German.

I did think him Englishman.

He is of the Saxony side.

He speak the french very well.

Tough he is German, he speak so much well italyan, french, spanish and english, that among the Italyans, they believe him Italyan, he speak the frenche as the Frenches himselves. The Spanishesmen believe him Spanishing, and the Englishes, Englishman.

It is difficult to enjoy well so much several langages.

Figure 5.6: From Carolino, P. (1883) *English as she is spoke*

Multilingual contexts: see page 10

This activity may be interesting and entertaining for Type A classes, but its learning potential is decreased if the errors caused by language transfer come from many different languages. It can be used in Type B classes if there is a language which all the students share, even if the teacher does not speak this language.

6   Language skills

It is probably the case that most teachers who use their students' own language as an important part of English language learning do so in activities that focus on discrete items of language, such as vocabulary or grammar (see Chapter 7). The students' own language can, however, be used economically and effectively to facilitate the development of the 'four skills' (reading, writing, listening, speaking). In addition, it lends itself to integrated skills work, as can be seen from a number of the activities in this chapter.

Translation, itself, could be also regarded as a language skill. Some writers, such as Maurice Claypole describe it as the fifth skill, 'the vital skill of negotiating between two languages' (Claypole, 2010). This is not the same as professional translating or interpreting, or even the kind of translation required for many philology courses at university: it is simply part and parcel of the day-to-day business of communicating with speakers of other languages. This, too, is reflected in a number of the activities in this chapter. These activities are intended primarily for language learners, rather than students following a translation course, although the latter will also benefit.

In conjunction with the activities described in this chapter, I would recommend teachers to look again at the basic techniques outlined in Chapter 2. Techniques 2.1: *Sandwiching*; 2.2: *Giving instructions*; 2.3: *Own-language moments*, and 2.4: *Language monitoring*, can all help learners with the development of their listening skills. Techniques 2.3 and 2.4 can help with speaking, not least in building confidence. I would also recommend revisiting the tools described in Chapter 4, most of which are especially helpful when it comes to reading and writing.

Glossaries

The provision of language support for learners in the development of their speaking and writing skills has long been standard practice. This may take the form of exercises, prior to the speaking or writing task, which focus on the language that the learners will need for the particular task: functional language, discourse markers, set phrases, etc. More simply, the tasks may be accompanied by 'Useful language' boxes. At lower levels especially, judicious use of the learners' own language may facilitate this kind of work.

With reading and listening skills, however, the provision of language support is much less generally accepted. A student's use of a dictionary or a recording script, for example, is often considered tantamount to cheating: students are usually expected to learn to tolerate partial understanding and to deduce meaning from context. It is understandable that teachers want to discourage the common learner practice of looking up every other word in a dictionary while reading a text ... and then rapidly forgetting these words. In listening practice, since students can rarely determine the speed at which they must listen, they do not in any case have the time to use a dictionary.

Recent researchers in reading skills (Grabe, 2008) and listening skills (Field, 2009) suggest that it may be time for a rethink in our approaches to reading and listening skills. The main problem that students have with reading is that they do not know enough words. Making more words more comprehensible (for example, through the provision of short glossaries, produced for specific texts and visible alongside them) may actually help to promote, not hinder, the development of reading skills. With lower levels, it may be more economical and more effective to use bilingual glossaries. One of the biggest problems that learners have with listening is also a lack of words, and this problem is compounded by difficulties with the recognition of word boundaries. Once again, glossaries may help.

Besides saving learners the chore of looking up words in a dictionary, glossaries may also promote the kind of hypothesis formation that some writers (e.g. Willis & Willis, 1996) consider essential to language acquisition. Look, for example, at the three Latin phrases below:

> *Repetitio est mater studiorum* (Repetition is the mother of study *or* Practice makes perfect)
> *Experientia docet* (Experience teaches *or* Experience is the best teacher)
> *Docendo discimus* (By teaching, we learn *or* We learn from teaching)

If you knew very little Latin and you were asked to translate them, you would be able to guess the meaning of a few words because of their similarity to English, but this would not get you very far with the second two phrases. You would soon need to start looking up words in a dictionary. The time spent doing this would be better spent doing something more useful. With a glossary that told you that *docere = to teach* and *discere = to learn*, you could quickly begin to make informed hypotheses about the meanings of the complete phrases. In the same way, glossaries (monolingual or bilingual) can encourage learners to become language detectives.

It is noticeable in recent years that some coursebooks have started to include glossaries alongside the texts and tasks for reading and listening work. Where these do not exist, it is easy for teachers to provide their own glossaries on the board. Decisions about whether these should be monolingual or bilingual will be best made by the teacher for each different group of students. Teachers can also decide whether these glossaries should give dictionary definitions/translations ('priming' glossaries) or definitions/translations of the words and phrases in the particular context in which they have been used ('prompting' glossaries) (Widdowson, 1978).

Video and multimedia

The increasing availability of online video and audio material has opened up a huge number of possibilities for language learners and teachers. The most frequently exploited are the opportunities for reading and listening (with video increasingly replacing audio recordings on CD). But with the growing potential of interactive, multimedia applications, opportunities for speaking, writing and integrated skills are also becoming more popular.

Two exciting developments for integrated skills work use video and translation as the basis for writing and speaking work. In Activity 6.14: *Writing subtitles*, students work collaboratively to make own-language subtitles. A European Commission funded project, 'Learning via Subtitling' (LeVIS, 2008), has made subtitling software available, along with suggestions for use. The dubbing of videos into the students' own language is more challenging, but can also lead to high levels of student engagement. Danan (2010) offers plenty of suggestions for teachers who wish to explore this option.

References

Claypole, M. (2010) 'Learners are getting lost without translation skills', *Guardian Weekly* 15 June. Available online at: www.guardian.co.uk/education/2010/jun/15/learners-are-getting-lost-without-translation. [Last accessed 01 July 2013]

Danan, M. (2010) 'Dubbing projects for the language learner: a framework for integrating audiovisual translation into task-based instruction', *Computer Assisted Language Learning*, Volume 23, Issue 5, pp. 441–56.

Field, J. (2009) *Listening in the Language Classroom*, Cambridge: Cambridge University Press.

Grabe, W. (2008) *Reading in a Second Language: Moving from theory to practice*, Cambridge: Cambridge University Press.

LeVIS Project Workshop (2008) Available online at: http://levis.cti.gr. [Last accessed 20 August 2013]

Widdowson, H. (1978) *Teaching Language as Communication*, Oxford: Oxford University Press.

Willis, D. & Willis, J. (1996) 'Consciousness-raising Activities' in Willis, D. & J. (eds.) *Challenge and Change in Language Teaching*, Oxford: Macmillan. Available online at: http://www.willis-elt.co.uk/books.html. [Last accessed 01 July 2013]

6.1 Preparing students for a text (content)

Outline	Students read or listen to a text or texts in their own language or in English as preparation for reading or listening in English.
Level	A2–B1
Time	15 minutes
Preparation	This activity is intended for use before students read (or listen to) a text which contains factual information. In coursebooks, factual, informative texts tend to be reading texts rather than the recorded listenings (which are more often conversations between invented people that have been scripted to illustrate a particular language point). The procedure is also a useful way of preparing learners for authentic texts (either spoken or written). Before the lesson, (1) make up a title for the text if it does not already have one, and (2) prepare a very brief synopsis of the text (see the examples in Figure 6.1 on page 97).

Procedure

1   Tell the students that they are going to read (or listen to) a text in English. Give them the title of the text and a brief synopsis: these can be written on the board or dictated.
2   Tell the students that their task is to research the topic of the text before they read it. They should do their research online and they can use websites in any language. If they use an English-language site, they can use online translation tools if they wish. They do not need to take notes, but they must be ready to talk about what they have learned.

   The students should spend about ten minutes on this task. If there is no online access in the classroom, the task can be set as homework.
3   Organise the class into small groups (two to four students). Tell them to spend five minutes sharing what they have learned. This can be done in their own language or in English, or in a mixture of the two. The primary purpose of the activity is to develop the students' background knowledge of the topic in order to help them with the reading (or listening). This may be better achieved in their own language, but if it can be done in English (i.e. with stronger, more confident learners), so much the better.
4   If you wish to prepare the students for the English vocabulary of the text, follow the procedure of Activity 6.2: *Preparing students for a text (vocabulary)*, at this stage. If not, move on to Stage 5.
5   Ask the students to read (or listen to) the text. If it is a text from a coursebook, you may want to use the tasks that accompany it. If it is an authentic piece of material, you may want to set your own tasks to guide their reading (or listening).

Title: The world's most unusual hotels

Synopsis: Travel writers describe their experiences of staying at the Hostel Celica in Ljubljana (Slovenia) and the Magic Mountain Hotel in the Huilo Huilo nature reserve (Chile)

Title: The Gucci Story

Synopsis: A brief history of the Gucci fashion house

Title: Banksy – graffiti artist

Synopsis: Biographical information about this artist

Figure 6.1: Examples referring to texts in *face2face Second Edition* Pre-intermediate by Redston, C. & Cunningham, G. (Cambridge University Press) pp. 58–9, 82, 99

Note
This activity can be combined with Activity 6.11: *Text expansion*.

Variation
Essentially the same procedure to generate ideas can be used to prepare students for a speaking or writing activity. The students research the topic using online resources in either their own language or in English, share their ideas with other students, and then plan what they are going to say or write. Using the students' own language in this way opens up the number of possible topics for both speaking and writing activities with lower-level classes. Movies, TV programmes, sports events/ commentaries, magazine and newspaper articles, websites, brochures (e.g. tourist guides), and texts related to the students' other academic subjects all become potential springboards for speaking or writing activities.

Multilingual contexts: see page 10
This activity can be used with both Type A and Type B classes.

6.2 Preparing students for a text (vocabulary)

Outline	Students brainstorm vocabulary (in English and their own language) as preparation for reading or listening in English. The activity can be used in conjunction with Activity 6.1: *Preparing students for a text (content)*.
Level	A2+
Time	Approximately 12 minutes
Preparation	This activity is intended for use before students read (or listen to) a text. The activity works best for texts which contain factual information: in coursebooks, these are more commonly reading (rather than listening) texts. However, the procedure is also a useful way of preparing learners for authentic texts (either spoken or written).
	Before the lesson, (1) make up a title for the text if it does not already have one, and (2) prepare a very brief synopsis of the text (see the examples given in Activity 6.1: *Preparing students for a text (content)*).

Procedure

1 Tell the students that they are going to read (or listen to) a text in English. Give them the title of the text and a brief synopsis: these can be written on the board or dictated.

2 Elicit from the class two or three words that they think will appear in the text. Write these on the board. Accept words in the students' own language. It may help to give two or three examples yourself first.

3 Tell the students to work individually and write down as many further words they can think of that they think they will encounter in the text. These words may be in English or in their own language. If necessary, point out that their lists should not contain words like the, have, from, be, etc. Set a time limit of three or four minutes.

   As a slight variation to this procedure, say that the words must be in English and set a time limit of two minutes. After two minutes, say that they may now add words in their own language. Allow another two minutes.

4 Organise the class into pairs. The students should compare their lists. Using any resources that are available, the students should first translate any words in their own language into English. They should then combine their lists to form one list of a maximum of ten words: this list should contain the words that they are most confident will appear in the text.

5 Ask the students to read (or listen to) the text. If it is a text from a coursebook, you may want to use the tasks that accompany it. If it is an authentic piece of material, you may want to set your own tasks to guide their reading (or listening).

Variation

The same procedure can be used to prepare students for speaking and writing tasks.

Multilingual contexts: see page 10

This activity can be used with both Type A and Type B classes.

6.3 Bilingual word clouds

Outline	Students use bilingual word clouds to study a text.
Level	A2+
Time	Variable (depending on length of text and level of learners)
Preparation	You will need parallel written texts, one in English, the other in the students' own language (see note on page 100). The English text could be from the students' coursebook, from published supplementary material, or be authentic. Paste one of these texts into the text field in a word-cloud program. Once the word cloud has been generated, you can change the font, colour and layout. Save or print the image, and then repeat the procedure with the other version of the text. You will also need copies of the English text.

Procedure

1 Introduce the topic of the lesson (in this example, it is the 2003 film *Lost in Translation*). If it is a topic that you think they will know something about, they can brainstorm what they know, and then compare information. If you think the topic will be unfamiliar, give them some more information about it (in this example, information about the directors, the stars and the plot), and if possible show a relevant picture or a short video clip.

2 Show the students the word cloud in their own language. Explain that the word cloud includes the content words of a text they are going to read. In the example below (Figure 6.2), an article about the film *Lost in Translation* has been used to create the word cloud. Ask the students to use the word cloud to predict what the text says. This should be done quickly and in the students' own language.

3 Hand out the text. Students compare the text to their predictions.

4 Tell the students to put the text out of sight. Hand out the English word cloud. In pairs, students compare the two word clouds and recall as much of the text as possible in English.

5 These activities can be followed (in this example) with a video clip of the movie trailer or an extract from the film. If the text used was only the beginning of a text, the students should then read the complete text.

Figure 6.2: Word clouds (Wordle) on the plot of *Lost in Translation* (2003)

Note

Suitable texts for this activity include factual/encyclopaedic texts (similar to the one used above), news items and sports reports, narratives and the beginnings of narratives, blog entries / opinion pieces, and song lyrics / poems. For lower level students (A2–B1), texts under 200 words will probably work best. It is a good idea to build up a stock of interesting parallel texts. Word-cloud programs include:

- Wordle (www.wordle.net)
- Tagxedo (www.tagxedo.com)
- Worditout (www.worditout.com)
- Tagcrowd (www.tagcrowd.com).

Multilingual contexts: see page 10

This activity cannot be used with Type A classes. It can be used in Type B classes if there is a language which all the students share, even if the teacher does not speak this language. However, the activity works much less well with languages that are highly inflected.

6.4 Bilingual parallel texts (reading and listening)

Outline	Students read a text in English while simultaneously hearing a translation of it. Alternatively, they listen to a text in English while simultaneously reading a translation of it.
Level	A1–B1
Time	4–5 minutes for the parallel reading/listening (depending on the length of the text)
Preparation	Select a text that you want the class to study. Prepare a translation of this text in the students' own language.

Procedure

1   Prepare the students for the text with a discussion related to the content or by brainstorming background knowledge or related vocabulary (see Activities 6.1: *Preparing students for a text (content)* and 6.2: *Preparing students for a text (vocabulary)*).

2   If you wish to set a reading task (e.g. the initial reading task suggested by the coursebook, if the text comes from a coursebook), do so now. Allow a suitable amount of time for students to do the task.

3   Before conducting feedback on the task, read aloud the translation of the text. Tell the students to listen and to follow the English text at the same time. This requires some concentration from the students. Read the text slowly, with pauses between phrases and sentences.

4   Ask the class if they want to hear the translation again. If they do, read it once more, at a slightly faster speed.

5   Allow the students to work with a partner to compare their answers to the task (if you have set one), and then conduct feedback.

6   Continue the lesson by setting any other tasks that are related to the text. You may wish to conclude the section of the lesson that is related to the text by reading the translation once more.

Variation

This technique can also be used with spoken texts. The activity works best if the translation of the spoken text is projected onto the board sentence by sentence, rather than given to the students as a photocopy, as the availability of the entire translation will distract from the listening. It is also better for the teacher to read the text aloud, rather than play a recording, as this allows for a better control of the speed of delivery. For teachers lacking confidence in their ability to do this well, a recording of a proficient speaker may be an alternative.

Multilingual contexts: see page 10

This activity cannot be used with Type A classes and it is inappropriate for Type B classes.

6.5 Note taking and summarising

Outline	Students listen to (or read) a text in English, take notes, and produce a summary in their own language.
Level	A2+
Time	Variable
Preparation	Select a text which the students will use. This could be a written text which you will read aloud or a recorded text (e.g. authentic material or a recording from a coursebook). Monologues or interviews where the interviewer says very little work best for this activity. The text should be no more than two minutes long for level A2, or about four minutes for level B1.

Procedure

1   Tell the class that they are going listen to a text in English. They will hear the text twice. Tell the class that their task will be to produce a short written summary. They should take notes when they are listening. If necessary, remind them not to attempt to transcribe entire sentences. These notes can be in English or in their own language if they prefer.

2   After the first listening, give the students a few minutes to compare their notes. Then, tell them to listen again.

3   The students should again be allowed some time to compare notes. It is a good idea, on this occasion, for them to compare their notes with a different student.

4   If you think it is necessary for the students to listen a third time, allow them to do so. If not, put the students into pairs and tell them to prepare a short, written summary of what they have heard. The summary should be in their own language, and they may discuss their ideas in their own language, too. Set a time limit: five minutes is usually enough, but you may wish to shorten this slightly in order to motivate them to work more quickly.

5   Ask the class if they wish to hear the text another time. If so, allow them to do so and give an extra minute or two afterwards in case they want to make any changes to their summary. If not, continue to the next stage.

6   Combine two pairs of students to form groups of four. Tell them to work together and, comparing their summaries, to produce a final version of their summary.

7   Ask two or three students to read their summaries aloud to the rest of the class. Ask the class which summary they prefer and their reasons for saying so. Discuss any issues which arise.

Variation

This activity can also be used with written texts. Rather than taking notes, students should be instructed to underline or highlight key words or phrases.

Multilingual contexts: see page 10

This activity can be used with both Type A and Type B classes.

6.6 Jumbled glossaries

Outline	Students match translations of words and phrases to their English equivalents in a text.
Level	A1+
Time	Approximately 10 minutes
Preparation	This activity is intended as a follow-up to an English text which the students have already begun to study in class (e.g. a text in their coursebooks). Select five or six words or phrases in the text which you think will be unfamiliar to the majority of the students. Find equivalents for these words and phrases in the students' own language.

Procedure

1   Make sure that everyone in the class has read the text at least twice and that they have a reasonable understanding of it. For this, you may wish to set first a task which requires students to read for gist, followed by a second task that requires a more detailed reading.
2   Take your list of words or phrases which you think will be unfamiliar to the majority of the students. Read these out aloud, one by one, and tell the students to find and underline them in the text.
3   Dictate the own-language equivalents of the words or phrases that the students have just underlined. (Alternatively, you can write them on the board.) Do this in a different order from the order which appears in the text.
4   Tell the class that they must match the underlined words in the text to the translations. Give them a few minutes to work on this individually, before allowing them to work with a partner.
5   Conduct feedback with the whole class.

Variations

1   If you wish to increase the degree of challenge/difficulty, either (1) tell the students to underline more items than there are translations for, or (2) dictate more 'translations' than there are underlined items. The creation of distractors of this kind will force the students to re-read the text more closely.
2   If you wish to further increase the degree of challenge/difficulty, do not tell the students which words to underline. This will force them to read the text very intensively to find English words and phrases that match the translations.
3   Instead of telling students to underline words in the text and dictating the own-language equivalents, the exercise can be prepared as a worksheet and photocopied.

Multilingual contexts: see page 10

This activity cannot be used if the teacher does not share a language, other than English, with the students.

6.7 Selecting appropriate translations for words or phrases in a text

Outline	Students use dictionaries to prepare a multiple choice vocabulary exercise that focuses on words in a text. They then exchange exercises and complete them.
Level	A2+
Time	Approximately 20 minutes (for about six items, but the time can be greater or less depending on the level of the class)
Preparation	Students need access to dictionaries. This activity is intended as a follow-up to an English text which the students have already begun to study in class (e.g. a text in their coursebooks). No further preparation is necessary unless the teacher prepares the exercise (see *Variation*).

Procedure

1 Make sure that everyone in the class has read the text at least twice and that they have a reasonable understanding of it. For this, you may wish to set first a task which requires students to read for gist, followed by a second task that requires a more detailed reading.

2 Organise the class into pairs. Half of the pairs should look at the first part of the text; the other half should look at the second part. You will need to be very clear about where these parts begin and end. Each pair should work with a bilingual dictionary. The students must select about six words from their text, which they should look up in their dictionaries. When they find a word that has more than one translation, they should note down these translations on a piece of paper (not more than three translations per word) along with the word in English. If there is only one translation for a word they have selected, they should move on and select another word. See the example on page 105 (Figure 6.3) using Spanish translations for how this works in practice.

3 The pairs should exchange the sheets of paper they have prepared with another pair that has been working with a different portion of the text. The students should look at the list of English words with their multiple translations, refer to the text, and select the best option or options. Sometimes, more than one of the translations will be possible in the context.

4 Conduct feedback with the whole class. Answer any queries the students may have.

Variation

With lower-level classes (A2), it is usually better for teachers to prepare the exercise themselves. In this case, the whole class works on the same exercise. This is more productive when students are working in pairs.

A number of sporting events in Britain are national institutions. Some are popular occasions, attended by thousands of spectators from all levels of society and watched on television by millions. Others are elegant and exclusive outdoor parties for the rich and their friends, where sport is secondary to social enjoyment. The Cup Final is an example of one extreme, Ascot of the other. Some, such as Wimbledon, are an interesting mixture of both.

Most of these events are attended by members of the Royal Family as well as by politicians, film stars, singers and business people. The venues are equipped with luxurious 'hospitality suites', used by companies to promote their business and thank important clients for their loyalty. Tickets for most of these events can be expensive, but not usually beyond the reach of ordinary people. They are often hard to find, however, as space is limited and there is great demand.

There are, of course, hundreds more events which draw large crowds – notably in football, cricket, golf, sailing and motor-racing – and everyone has their favourites. The historical traditions, the holiday atmosphere, and the pleasure and excitement of the spectators (often with an element of suspense provided by the weather) make these some of the most enjoyable and friendly occasions of the year.

Spanish Translations

event	acontecimiento, suceso, acto
attend	acudir, asistir, atender
party	fiesta, partido, grupo
venue	lugar, local, campo
promote	fomentar, promover, promocionar
draw	dibujar, empatar, atraer

Figure 6.3: From Collie, J. & Martin, A. (2000) *What's It Like?*, Cambridge: Cambridge University Press, p. 24

Multilingual contexts: see page 10

This activity cannot be used with Type A classes. It can be used effectively with Type B classes: it is not necessary for the teacher to use any language other than English.

6.8 Translation problems

Outline	Students analyse a text for translation difficulties, then compare their ideas and work together on resolving these problems.
Level	A2+
Time	15 minutes + (depending on the level of the class, and the length and degree of difficulty of the text)
Preparation	This activity is intended as a follow-up to an English text which the students have already studied in class (e.g. a text in their coursebooks). No further preparation is necessary.

Procedure

1 Make sure that everyone in the class has read the text at least twice and that they have a reasonable understanding of it. For this, you may wish to set first a task which requires students to read for gist, followed by a second task that requires a more detailed reading.

2 Ask students to look at the text again and to underline anything (words or phrases) that they think they would find difficult to translate into their own language. At this stage, they do not have to translate anything, although they will be translating *mentally* as they do the task. With higher levels (B2+), draw the students' attention to the style of the text. Students should work individually. Set a time limit for this: three or four minutes is enough for a text of approximately 200 words at B1 level.

3 Organise the class into pairs or groups of three. Students compare their underlined words and phrases, and help each other, where possible, to resolve any difficulties. At this stage they should not refer to dictionaries or other aids.

4 Tell the class that they can now refer to dictionaries or other aids (1) to check their work, and (2) to attempt to resolve any outstanding difficulties. The students remain in their pairs or groups for this task.

5 Conduct feedback with the whole class. First, identify those parts of the text that a majority of the students found problematic. Then, check whether satisfactory solutions have been found. Finally, resolve any difficulties that are still outstanding.

6 Some teachers then ask the class (either individually or in pairs/groups) to translate the whole text. This is often set as homework.

Multilingual contexts: see page 10

This activity can be used with both Type A and Type B classes.

6.9 Intensive reading (or listening) with translation

Outline Students compare an English text with a translation to identify differences between them.
Level All levels
Time Approximately 10 minutes
Preparation This activity is intended as a follow-up to an English text which the students have already studied in class (e.g. a text in their coursebooks). Prepare a translation of a part of this text into the students' own language. Six sentences are usually enough for the activity, but with higher levels a longer amount of text could be used. These sentences could be from anywhere within the text or they could be one paragraph. Include in your translation five or six differences from the English version (i.e. not grammatical mistakes in the students' language, but minor changes to content or vocabulary).

Procedure

1 Make sure that everyone in the class has read the text at least twice and that they have a reasonable understanding of it. For this, you may wish to set first a task which requires students to read for gist, followed by a second task that requires a more detailed reading.
2 Dictate the sentences to the students (in their own language).
3 Ask the students to find the corresponding English sentences in the text.
4 Tell the students how many translation problems they need to identify; there are six in the example (Figure 6.4) below, translated from German. Tell them to compare the translation with the original text and find the problems.
5 Allow students to compare their answers with a partner before conducting feedback with the whole class.

German translation of text with six changes

Jedem von uns wird beigebracht, dass man nicht lügen soll. Aber es scheint, dass jeder Lügen erzählt – nicht nur tatsächliche Lügen, sondern das, was man Notlügen nennt. Obwohl wir wissen, dass man nicht lügen soll, warum machen wir es dann so oft? Meistens gibt es nachvollziehbare Gründe zu lügen, zum Beispiel um einen Freund zu schützen oder jemandes Gefühle. Also, wann lügen wir und wen lügen wir an?

Text with six changes

All of us are taught to believe that lying is wrong. But it seems that everybody tells lies – not only big lies, but what we call 'white lies'. If we know that lying is wrong, why do we do it so much? Most of the time, people have understandable reasons for lying. For example, they might want to protect a friend or someone's feelings. So, when do we lie and who to?

Original text

Most of us are taught to believe that lying is wrong. But it seems that everybody tells lies – not big lies, but what we call 'white lies'. If we believe that lying is wrong, why do we do it? Most of the time, people have very good reasons for lying. For example, they might want to protect a friendship or someone's feelings. So, when do we lie and who to?

Figure 6.4: From Richards, J. C. with Hull, J. & Proctor, S. (2005) *Interchange 2 Third Edition*, Cambridge: Cambridge University Press, p. 111

Variation

A version of this activity provides learners with listening practice.

1 Prepare an anecdote or short story that you think would interest the class. It is not necessary to script this, but it would be helpful to make a few notes.
2 Tell the class the anecdote or story using the students' language.
3 Tell the class that they will hear the story again, this time in English. Tell them that there will be certain factual differences between this version and the version that they heard previously. Tell the story, but include a small number of factual differences (five or six are usually enough). Speak naturally; use paraphrases if students do not understand any unfamiliar words or phrases, and repeat key sections, if necessary.
4 Organise the class into pairs. Give the students time to compare their ideas before conducting feedback with the whole class.

Multilingual contexts: see page 10

This activity cannot be used if the teacher does not share a language, other than English, with the students.

6.10 Mixed language listening

Outline	Students listen to a text, part of which is in English and part of which is in their own language.
Level	A1–B1
Time	Approximately 15 minutes
Preparation	Prepare an anecdote or short story (no more than about two minutes long) that you think would interest the class. It is not necessary to script this, but it would be helpful to make a few notes. Make a mental note of the mid-point of the story.

Procedure

1 Tell the class that you are going to tell them a story. Begin by telling the story in the students' own language. At the mid-point of the story, switch into English.
2 Organise the class into pairs. The students tell each other what they can remember.
3 Tell the class the story again. This time, switch the languages (i.e. use English for the first part of the story, and the students' own language for the second part).
4 The students work in pairs again and repeat Stage 2.
5 With the whole class, elicit the story, sentence by sentence, from individual students. Encourage the use of English only, but if some phrases remain difficult for students to express in English, write these own-language phrases on the board. When the story has been completed, return to the phrases that are not in English and suggest ways of translating them.

Variation

Instead of telling the first part of the story in the students' own language and the second part in English, the teacher can also alternate between languages between sentences.

Note

I first came across the idea of code-switching in listening practice in Deller, S. & Rinvolucri, M. (2002) *Using the Mother Tongue*, Peaslake: Delta Publishing, p. 57. They, in turn, acknowledge Peter Grundy as the source of their idea.

Multilingual contexts: see page 10

This activity cannot be used if the teacher does not share a language, other than English, with the students.

6.11 Text expansion

Outline	Students extend an English text after researching the topic in their own language.
Level	A1–B1
Time	Approximately 30 minutes
Preparation	This activity is intended as a follow-up to an English text which the students have already studied in class (e.g. a text in their coursebooks). No further preparation is needed. Students will need online access in the classroom, but if this is not available, they can do the research as a homework assignment.

This activity can easily be combined with Activity 6.1: *Preparing students for a text (content)*.

Procedure

1 Make sure that everyone in the class has read the text at least twice and that they have a good understanding of it.

2 Tell the students that their task will be to extend the text. First, if they have not already done so (see Activity 6.1: *Preparing students for a text (content)*), they should further research the topic of the text. They should do their research online and they can use websites in any language. If they use an English-language site, they can use online translation tools if they wish. They do not need to take notes, but they must find out at least five additional pieces of information which could be added to the text.

   Tell them that they should spend about ten minutes on this task. If there is no online access in the classroom, this task can be set as homework.

3 Organise the class into pairs. Tell the pairs to spend four or five minutes sharing what they have learnt. They must (1) select at least five pieces of information which they can add to the text, (2) decide where in the text this information can be inserted.

   This can be done in their own language or in English, or in a mixture of the two. The primary purpose of the activity is to make sure they have enough content ideas to have something to write about. This may be better achieved in their own language, but if it can be done in English (i.e. with stronger, more confident students), so much the better.

4 On the board, give an example of what you want the students to do. Elicit one additional piece of information from the class (or provide one of your own), decide where and how it could be inserted in the text, and write this on the board (see the example in Figure 6.5 on page 111). Point out that the insertion of extra information may require little changes to the sentences around the insertion (as in the example).

5 The pairs complete the writing extension task. Allow the students to use dictionaries.

6 The pairs exchange their new, expanded texts with those of other pairs. They read each other's work.

The smallest independent country in the world, the Vatican City covers an area the size of a golf course in Rome, the capital of Italy. It was founded in 1929 and is ruled by just one man, the Pope, who is also the head of the Catholic Church. **The current Pope, Francis, comes from Argentina. ~~Its~~ The Vatican's** buildings – such as St Peter's ...

The Vatican City

The smallest independent country in the world, the Vatican City covers an area the size of a golf course in Rome, the capital of Italy. It was founded in 1929 and is ruled by just one man, the Pope, who is also the head of the Catholic Church. Its buildings – such as St Peter's Basilica and the Sistine Chapel – are home to some of the world's most famous art, including works by Botticelli, Raphael and Michelangelo.

The Vatican has its own bank, army, police force, fire brigade, post office, satellite TV channel, radio station and internet domain (.va). The Vatican army, called the Swiss Guard, is the smallest in the world. It has about 100 soldiers, all unmarried, and all from Switzerland. The Vatican postal service has an excellent reputation: an international letter posted in the Vatican will arrive faster than one dropped just a few hundred metres away in Italy.

Millions of people visit the Vatican every year, but the Vatican has a population of only about 800 people. The Vatican has no official language. The Swiss Guard use German, but most people use Italian and Latin. In fact, the Vatican's bank machines are the only ones in the world that give instructions in Latin.

The country's economy is unique. It receives most of its money from Catholics around the world and from tourism. It also makes money from a petrol station where Italians can buy fuel 30 percent more cheaply than in Italy – because the Vatican has no taxes!

ROME

Figure 6.5: From Tilbury, A., Clementson, T., Hendra, L. & Rea, D. (2010) *English Unlimited B1*, Cambridge: Cambridge University Press, p. 99

Multilingual contexts: see page 10

This activity can be used with both Type A and Type B classes.

6.12 Watching videos with English and own-language subtitles

Outline	Students watch an English-language video clip and discuss what they have seen and heard.
Level	B1+
Time	20 minutes + (depending on the length and complexity of the clip)
Preparation	You will need to select a video clip that will interest your students. The video needs to be available in three versions: with English subtitles, with own-language subtitles and without subtitles. Some commercially produced DVDs provide these three options in their 'language' and 'subtitles' menus. Alternatively, you may find three versions of the same clip at video-sharing websites such as YouTube.

The clip should not be more than three or four minutes long (for a B1 group), but more advanced students can work with longer clips.

Suggestions for sourcing suitable videos can be found in Ben Goldstein and Paul Driver's forthcoming *Language Learning with Digital Video* (Cambridge University Press, 2014).

Procedure

1 Prepare the students for the topic of the video through a short discussion related to the topic. Pre-teach any vocabulary (maximum five or six items) that will be essential to understanding the clip. Alternatively, provide the students with a glossary: this could be quickly written on the board.
2 Play the clip once with the sound down and no subtitles. The students work in pairs and discuss what they have seen. They should speak in English, but you may wish to permit some use of their own language (see Activity 2.3: *Own-language moments* and Activity 2.4: *Language monitoring*).
3 Play the clip again, this time with the sound up, but with no subtitles. The students again work in pairs and discuss what they have seen and heard, developing and modifying their ideas from the previous stage.
4 Play the clip a third time, this time with the sound up and with English subtitles. The students again work in pairs and discuss what they have seen and heard, developing and modifying their ideas from the previous stage.
5 Play the clip a final time, this time with the sound up and with subtitles in the students' own language.
6 Ask the class (1) how close their original ideas were to their final understanding, and (2) if they have any queries about the language of the clip.

Multilingual contexts: see page 10

This activity cannot be used with Type A classes. It can be used in Type B classes if there is a language which all the students share, even if the teacher does not speak this language.

6.13 Translations and dubbed videos

Outline	Students translate an extract from a film clip into their own language, and then compare their work with a dubbed version of the clip.
Level	B1+
Time	25 minutes + (depending on length and complexity of clip)
Preparation	You will need to select a video clip that will interest your students. The video needs to be available in both the original English-language version and dubbed into the students' own language. Most commercially produced DVDs (sold outside English-speaking countries) provide these options. You will also need photocopies of the transcript of the clip that you are going to use. These can often be found online by typing "(*name of movie*) + movie script" into a search engine. The clip should not be more than three or four minutes long (for a B1 group), but more advanced students can work with longer clips. Student access to dictionaries is desirable, but not necessary.

Procedure

1 Generate some interest in the movie clip that the students will be working with by discussing the topic, the story, the actors, etc.
2 Hand out photocopies of the transcript. Ask the students if they can identify which part of the film the extract comes from. Give the students a few minutes to read the texts.
3 Play the video clip in the original English version. The students watch and listen, and may also follow the dialogue on their photocopied transcripts.
4 Organise the students into pairs. Their task is to translate the transcript into their own language. They may consult dictionaries. Allow sufficient time for students to do this work, before putting pairs together to form groups of four which can compare their work.
5 Tell the class that you will now play the clip again. As they watch/listen, they should follow the dialogue in their translated version. Play the video clip in the dubbed version.
6 Conduct feedback with the whole class. Ask if any of the language in the dubbed version was very different from the English version or from their own translations. It is a good idea to note one or two differences yourself when you listen to the dubbed version. Students are usually more likely to make their own suggestions if you make one or two first.

Note

I first came across the potential of using dubbed film clips in Gonzalez Davies, M. (2004) *Multiple Voices in the Translation Classroom*, Amsterdam / Philadelphia: John Benjamins, p. 181.

Multilingual contexts: see page 10

This activity cannot be used with Type A classes. It can be used in Type B classes if there is a language which all the students share, even if the teacher does not speak this language.

6.14 Writing subtitles

Outline	Students prepare, produce and upload subtitled video clips.
Level	B1+
Time	20 minutes + (depending on length and complexity of clip)
Preparation	Before the lesson, negotiate with the class the choice of an English song they would like to work on. The song should be available as an online video (e.g. on YouTube). Download the lyrics of the song and make enough copies for each group in the class.

Procedure

1 Begin the activity with a short discussion about the song: what the students like or dislike about it, what they know about the performer, what it is about, etc.
2 Distribute the lyrics of the song and show the class a video of its performance.
3 Explain that they are going to subtitle the video clip in their own language.
4 Organise the class into groups. Each group works collaboratively to prepare their translation. Make bilingual dictionaries available and be prepared to help any groups that are struggling.
5 Reorganise the students so that the work of different groups can be compared, edited and improved.
6 Ask for one student volunteer to subtitle the video at home that evening. This is a very simple operation, and costs nothing. There is a captioning program available at www.captiontube.appspot.com.
7 The subtitled video can be watched in a subsequent class.

Notes

Many ELT websites (e.g. www.its-teachers.com/interact/songs) offer lists of pop songs suitable for classroom work of this kind. Students find this task particularly motivating if they can post their finished work onto a video-sharing site.

Variation

A low-tech alternative to inserting the subtitles into the video clip is a kind of *chuchotage* (whispered interpreting). Chuchotage is a voice-over simultaneous translation that used to be widely employed in the television services of some countries. One speaker, and usually only one, provides a simultaneous translation, but the original voices are still audible.

In the classroom, this technique can be used instead of uploading the translated subtitles onto the video clip. One student comes to the front of the class and stands by the video screen while the clip is being played. The student reads aloud the prepared translation and attempts to synchronise, more or less, her/his reading with the voices on the screen. This can be very entertaining, but it is also a challenging task.

Other short video clips are also suitable for this activity: trailers for upcoming films, short news bulletins, advertisements (especially funny ones), miscellaneous viral video clips, short interviews with celebrities, politicians, etc.

Multilingual contexts: see page 10

This activity cannot be used with Type A classes. It can be used in Type B classes if there is a language which all the students share, even if the teacher does not speak this language.

6.15 Bilingual role plays

Outline	Students practise speaking, listening and translating in three-way role plays.
Level	A1+
Time	10 minutes +
Preparation	This activity is a simple adaptation for any basic role play. Most coursebooks include role plays for the lower levels (up to B1) and these are often found alongside material that presents and practises functional language (e.g. suggesting, inviting, offering) or 'survival English'.

Procedure

1 If possible, prepare the students for the role play by getting them to listen to a model. In the example from a coursebook below (Figure 6.6), students listen to similar conversations and focus on some useful phrases.

2 Organise the class into groups of three (Students A, B and C). Hand out role cards to the A and B students in each group. Tell the C students that they are going to act as interpreters in a dialogue between a customer who cannot speak English and an English-speaking assistant in a small shop. Give all the students a few minutes to think silently about what they are going to say.

3 Tell the students to do the role play. Tell the A students (the customers in the example below) that they can only speak their own language and that Student C will interpret for them. Tell the B students that they can only speak English. Tell the C students that they can speak both languages.

4 When everyone has completed the role play, ask the class about any difficulties they encountered. Elicit or provide suggestions for getting round these difficulties.

5 ˙ Ask the students to change roles and repeat the role play.

Student A	Student B
You're a customer in a small shop. Tick (✓) three things you'd like to buy. postcards of Glasgow stamps a drink a local newspaper a sandwich a phone card You'd like to pay by card. You have cash, but only a £50 note.	You're an assistant in a small shop. You sell: postcards of Glasgow 80p each books of 12 stamps £3.50 each local newspaper £1.20 each phone cards £5 or £10 each You don't have: drinks sandwiches You don't take cards, only cash. You don't want any big notes.

Figure 6.6: From Tilbury, A., Clementson, T., Hendra, L. & Rea, D. (2010) *English Unlimited B1*, Cambridge: Cambridge University Press, pp. 123, 129

Variation

As a variation on this activity, Maria Gonzalez Davies suggests that it is done through writing in Gonzalez Davies, M. (2004) *Multiple Voices in the Translation Classroom*, Amsterdam / Philadelphia: John Benjamins, p. 63.

Note

This activity lends itself particularly well to role plays where there is an intercultural encounter, such as a conversation between an American or British tourist (who can speak only English), a local and an interpreter about, for example:

- local food (e.g. a menu)
- a local festival
- meeting a business contact for the first time
- giving presents
- the rules of punctuality
- how to get a taxi.

For further suggestions, see Corbett, J. (2010) *Intercultural Language Activities*, Cambridge: Cambridge University Press.

Multilingual contexts: see page 10

This activity cannot be used with Type A classes. It can be used in Type B classes if there is a language which all the students share, even if the teacher does not speak this language.

6.16 Assisted listening

Outline	Students give an oral presentation to the class which is accompanied by a glossary they have prepared.
Level	All levels
Time	Variable
Preparation	None

Procedure

1 On a regular basis, arrange for individual students to give oral presentations to the rest of the class. These presentations could be related to dual language resources that the students have researched (see Activity 4.13: *Dual language resources exchange*), but could also be the students' work, studies, interests or other aspects of their lives. Tell the students that as part of their planning for the presentations, they must prepare a dual language glossary for words and phrases which they will use, and which they think the other students (who will be listening to their presentations) may not know. For a presentation of about five minutes, they should not use more than about ten words which they think may cause problems.

2 Before individual students begin their presentations ask them to write their glossary on the board. If possible, this should be done in the order in which the other members of the class will hear these words and phrases.

Variation

For higher-level (B2+) classes, instead of writing a full glossary before the presentation, ask students to write the English words or phrases and the own-language equivalents in a jumbled order. For even higher-level classes, only the own-language equivalents need be given (without any English phrases, jumbled or otherwise): these should be written in the order in which they will be heard. In addition to listening to the content of the presentation, the other students must also try to match the translations or identify the English words and phrases that have been use (see Activity 6.6: *Jumbled glossaries*).

Multilingual contexts: see page 10

This activity cannot be used with Type A classes. It can be used in Type B classes if there is a language which all the students share, even if the teacher does not speak this language.

6.17 Assisted translation

Outline	Students translate an English poem or a song lyric into their own language, using a bilingual glossary.
Level	A2+
Time	Variable (depending on length of poem or song)
Preparation	Select a poem or a song lyric which you want the class to work on. It is important that the degree of grammatical difficulty is appropriate to the learners, but the range and difficulty of vocabulary is not important. Annotate the copy of the poem that you will distribute to the students with translations of all words that you think may be unfamiliar (see the example (Figure 6.7) on page 119).

Procedure

1 Generate some interest in the topic of the poem or song. In the example, students could be asked to (1) make a list of the things they miss when they are away from home, or (2) describe a moment when they have felt homesick.

2 Organise the class into pairs or small groups. Hand out photocopies of the annotated poem or project this onto the board. The students work together to produce a translation of the poem or song.

3 When everyone has finished, display the different translations so that they can be seen (e.g. on the walls of the classroom). Each student should read as many of these versions as possible.

4 Work through the poem with the whole class, writing up one acceptable version on the board as you go. Resolve any queries about acceptability or accuracy.

5 With some poems and songs, a possible follow-up is to ask the students to change words in phrases in the text so that the poem or song is more amusing / sadder / more personally true, etc.

Multilingual contexts: see page 10

This activity cannot be used if the teacher does not share a language, other than English, with the students.

Like a Beacon

In London
every now and then
I get this craving
for my mother's food
I leave art galleries
in search of plantains
saltfish / sweet potatoes

I need this link

I need this touch
of home
swinging my bag
like a beacon
against the cold

Grace Nichols

French translations

craving n   C désir ardent •*have a craving for sth* être assoiffé de qqch
plantain n   C banane des Antilles, plantain
saltfish n   C/U morue salée
link n   C lien, maillon
swing v   balancer, faire balancer
beacon n   C phare, balise

Figure 6.7: Poem reproduced by permission from Grace Nichols

7   Language focus

The previous chapter looked at classroom activities where use of the students' own language contributed, in some way, to practice in using English. This chapter looks at activities where particular elements of English (such as vocabulary and grammar) are studied through a comparison with the learners' language. The belief that contrasting particular features of a target language (in our case, English) and the learners' own language can help the learner to acquire the former is one that has generated much debate.

Over fifty years ago, Robert Lado argued in his influential *Linguistics across Cultures: Applied linguistics for language teachers* that features of a foreign language that are similar to a student's native language will be easy to learn, and those that are different will be harder. Therefore, he reasoned, a teacher who has contrasted the two languages 'will know better what the real learning problems are and can better provide for teaching them' (Lado, 1957, p. 2). At the time, many, if not most, people agreed with him. One was the eminent linguist, Michael Halliday. While rejecting some traditional practices, such as the translation of isolated decontextualised sentences and the learning of word lists with translation equivalents, Halliday argued against those who were convinced that one should not pay attention to the learner's mother tongue. 'Given the right conditions,' he wrote, 'one can make positive use of the student's mother tongue; and in such cases to neglect it may be to throw away one of the tools best adapted to the task in hand' (Halliday, 2007, p. 161).

Not so, responded the next generation of linguists, and their arguments won the day. Most of the mistakes that language learners make are not caused by interference (or crossover) from their first language, they claimed, and 'learners' first languages are no longer believed to interfere with their attempts to learn second language grammar' (Dulay et al., 1982, p. 5). Furthermore, it was argued, the use of translation in language learning actually caused mistakes through 'negative transfer' or 'first language interference'. Lado and the school of Contrastive Analysis, with which he was closely connected, became deeply unfashionable.

Who was right? The arguments of one generation of researchers, however convincing they may sound, tend to be questioned by the next. By the time that the critical consensus of researchers has been accepted by many classroom teachers, the critical research consensus has often moved on. The last ten years have seen another swing of the pendulum and a positive review of Lado's work by Claire Kramsch (2007), echoed by Michael Swan (2008), are indications of this swing.

Current perspectives

The current research consensus is reasonably clear. First of all, few researchers would now quarrel with the basic idea that the relationship between the learners' own language and the target language is important and unavoidable. Learners, as Henry Widdowson has put it, 'cannot be immunized against the influence of their own language, […] there is bound to be contact and […] language learning is indeed of its nature, in some degree, a compound bilingual experience' (Widdowson, 2003, pp. 151–2).

For vocabulary acquisition, Paul Nation (1997), among others, has shown that the study of bilingual word lists is indeed valuable, especially for the initial learning of new words and phrases. More recent research with teenagers has shown that approaches to the teaching of vocabulary which employ elements of translation and contrastive analysis can be more effective than approaches which eschew them (Laufer & Girsai, 2008). For some areas of vocabulary, such as false friends, it has been suggested that translation is essentially the only way of dealing with them. For the study of grammar, it would seem that some grammatical features (those that are subject to interference from the learners' own language) lend themselves particularly well to translation exercises. Since the particular areas of grammar which lend themselves to a contrastive approach vary from one learner's own language to another's, the activities suggested in this chapter are not specific to a particular feature of grammar: they can be used with virtually any feature. Scheffler (2012) reports research which supports contrastive analysis work (and translation) in grammar teaching. Scheffler concludes that the teachers who ignored the researchers, and carried on using translation in the classroom, were probably right all along.

How and how much

To what degree, and precisely how, language learning should be a 'compound bilingual experience' is problematic, and it is almost impossible to generalise answers to these questions. How, and how much, will depend on particular learning contexts: institutions, curricula, teachers and students, and even particular moments in lessons.

For the how, teachers are recommended first to look again at the basic techniques suggested in Chapter 2. The explanation or explication of language is likely to play an important role in any language-focused moments of teaching, and the techniques of sandwiching, recasting and own-language mirroring will all be useful. The techniques suggested in section 2.2: *Giving instructions,* can also be adapted to support learners' understanding of a teacher's explanations.

- Introduce grammatical metalanguage in English gradually, using the sandwich technique as you introduce it. Keep a record of such language that you have introduced for each class.
- Use wall displays of this language to help you and the students move towards less need for the students' own language.
- When you begin to give explanations in English only, ask students to repeat or summarise these in their own language.

A knowledge of the bilingual tools discussed in Chapter 4 (dictionaries, grammar books, word cards and other online resources) will also be invaluable to both teachers and learners. As noted above, this book does not offer suggestions for teaching approaches to particular areas of grammar, because those which lend themselves to a bilingual approach vary so much from one student language to another. However, a good bilingual reference resource will identify these areas, and usually suggest contrastive examples which can be explored and practised using the activities in this chapter and in Chapter 5.

The activities in this chapter all involve, to varying degrees, pair or group work. Whilst it would be possible to drop these episodes and adopt a more teacher-centred approach, this is not generally advisable. It is through the process of struggling to see the differences between English and their own language that learners will make progress, and this process is facilitated by interaction between the learners.

References

Dulay, H., Burt, M. & Krashen, S. (1982) *Language Two*, Oxford: Oxford University Press.

Halliday, M A K. (2007) *Language and Education* (ed. Jonathan J. Webster), London: Continuum.

Kramsch, C. (2007) 'Rereading Robert Lado' *International Journal of Applied Linguistics* 17, pp. 242–7.

Lado, R. (1957) *Linguistics across Cultures: Applied linguistics for language teachers*, Ann Arbor: University of Michigan Press.

Laufer, B. & Girsai, N. (2008) 'Form-focused instruction in second language vocabulary learning: a case for contrastive analysis and translation', *Applied Linguistics* 29, pp. 694–716.

Nation, P. (1997) 'L1 and L2 Use in the Classroom: A Systematic Approach', *TESL Reporter*, 30, 2, pp. 19–27.

Scheffler, P. (2012) 'Theories pass. Learners and teachers remain', *Applied Linguistics*, 33, 5, pp. 603–7.

Swan, M. (2008) 'History is not what happened: the case of Contrastive Analysis' Available online at: www.mikeswan.co.uk/elt-applied-linguistics/contrastive-analysis.htm. [Last accessed 01 July 2013]

Widdowson, H. (2003) *Defining Issues in English Language Teaching*, Oxford: Oxford University Press.

7.1 Words for free (true friends)

Outline	Students study lists of 'true friends' (English ↔ own language) and practise pronunciation.
Level	A1–B2
Time	Approximately 15 minutes
Preparation	Prepare a list of words that are cognates in English and the students' language (true friends). Organise these into parts of speech (nouns, verbs, adjectives, etc.) and, if possible, organise these further into smaller groups of words which share morphemes (e.g. prefixes, suffixes or word stems). See the example sets for German speakers on page 125 (Figure 7.1). Choose a group of seven to ten words each time that you want to use the activity. This activity can be repeated with different sets of words on a regular basis.

Procedure

1 Dictate the set of words to the students.
2 Students compare their answers with a partner, before looking at the correct spellings which are written on the board.
3 Drill the pronunciation of the English words.
4 Pronounce one of the words from the list, either in English or in the students' own language. Ask the students which language the word they heard was from. Do this with a few words so the students understand how the activity works. Once the procedure is clear, students can continue doing the same with a partner: one says a word from the list, the other says which language has been pronounced.
5 Elicit from the class (or point out, if necessary) any useful generalisations that can be made about these pairs of words. These might include predictable spelling changes, predictably different prefixes and suffixes, different stress patterns, ways of pronouncing individual letters or combinations of letters.
6 Elicit from the class (or suggest) any more words that can be added to the list. Learners should be encouraged to make guesses, but, of course, these will not always be correct!

	German	**English**
Miscellaneous international words (see also Activity 7.2: *Words for free (International Words)*	Rumpsteak Saxofon Shoppingcenter Shuttlebus Vitamin	rump steak saxophone shopping centre shuttle bus vitamin
Adjectives ending in *-al* (German) and *-al* (English)	international kolossal regional total trivial universal	international colossal regional total trivial universal
Adjectives ending in *-iv* (German) and *-ive* (English)	exklusiv explosiv expressiv figurativ innovativ intensiv	exclusive explosive expressive figurative innovative intensive
Nouns ending in *-ismus* (German) and *-ism* (English)	Anarchismus Faschismus Feudalismus Orientalismus Sozialismus Totalitarismus	anarchism fascism feudalism orientalism socialism totalitarianism
Words beginning with *k-* (German) and *c-* (English)	Kanal Katholik Korridor Krater Kreole Kristall	canal catholic corridor crater creole crystal
Proper nouns	Afrika Amerika Asien Australien Europa Mexiko	Africa America Asia Australia Europe Mexico

Figure 7.1: 'True friends' in English and German

Multilingual contexts: see page 10

This activity could be used with Type A classes if the words that are focused on are limited to international words. However, for that purpose, teachers may prefer to use Activity 7.2: *Words for free (international words)*. The activity can be used with Type B classes.

7.2 Words for free (international words)

Outline	Students study sets of international words and focus on pronunciation.
Level	A1–A2
Time	Approximately 20 minutes
Preparation	Prepare two sets of about seven international words (see the list below). Half the class will need a photocopy of one set, half the class will need the other set.
	The students will need access to online dictionaries (with a pronunciation feature) or dictionaries with phonemic transcriptions which the students can understand.
	This activity can be repeated with different sets of words on a regular basis.

Procedure

1 Explain to the class that they will be learning some words that are, more or less, the same in their language and in English. Organise the class into pairs. Distribute the word sets so that each student in a pair has a different set.

2 Demonstrate the activity to the class by selecting another international word. Using English (and mime and pictures, if necessary) elicit the word from the class. Tell the students that they must do the same. Give the students enough time to do the activity (about ten minutes is usually appropriate).

3 While still in pairs, tell the students to use their dictionaries to find out how the English words are pronounced. Tell them to mark any sounds which do not exist in their own language, any letters or combinations of letters that are different from the pronunciation in their own language, and the main stress in each word. They should also practise saying these words. This stage of the activity should take around ten minutes.

Sample list of international words

a look, app, bank, best of, bikini, blog, café, CD, champagne, chocolate, charter flight, clip, cool, cowboy, curry, design, DJ, download, DVD, email, fashion, fitness club, golf, hamburger, hotel, in (= fashionable), Internet, jazz, jeans, job, juice bar, leader, leggings, low cost, marketing, MBA, no fun, OK, post, pub, reboot, sauna, shopping, smartphone, smoothie, taxi, tennis, top (= item of clothing), T-shirt, video, yoga

Not all of these words can be used in all languages. You should be able to adapt and add to the list easily. Many lists can be found online by entering "cognates + English + *(students' own language)*" into a search engine.

Multilingual contexts: see page 10

This activity can be used with both Type A and Type B classes.

7.3 False friends

Outline	Students identify and research a set of false friends.
Level	A1–B2
Time	Approximately 20 minutes
Preparation	Prepare a list of false friends between English and the students' own language. Good bilingual dictionaries often provide lists of false friends, but they are usually easy to find by typing "false friends English + *(students' own language)*" into a search engine.

Choose a group of about seven words each time that you want to use this activity. Prepare a list of English sentences, each of which contains one of the false friends. Again, good monolingual or bilingualised dictionaries will provide appropriate sample sentences. See the example on page 128 (Figure 7.2) for speakers of Spanish. You will need to project these sentences onto the board or distribute photocopies.

As with Activity 7.1: *Words for free (true friends)*, this activity can be done with the class on a regular basis (with different sets of words).

Procedure

1 Distribute or project the sentences and ask the students to find one word in each sentence that looks like a word in their language, but has a very different meaning in English.
2 Ask students to compare their ideas with a partner and to guess (if they do not know) the own-language translations of the words they have identified. After giving them a few minutes to do this, ask them to check their answers in a dictionary.
3 Ask the pairs of students to produce two more sentences which include the target words. Then, elicit a few suggestions from the class and write these on the board.
4 Now ask the students to use their dictionaries to find the English equivalents for the false friends in their own language. In the example on page 128, these are *soportar, realizar, embarazada*, etc. Ask the pairs of students to produce two more sentences for each of these English equivalents. Then, elicit a few suggestions from the class and write these on the board.

Look at the sentences below. In each sentence, one word looks like a Spanish word, but its meaning in English is very different. Find the words.

1   He has to support six children.

2   I didn't realise that it was important.

3   She was very embarrassed when she made a mistake.

4   That centre assists the poor.

5   The doctor wanted to know if she was constipated.

6   The student went to a lecture about linguistics.

7   You can get that book out of a good library.

Key

support ≠ *soportar*; realise (*realize*) ≠ *realizar*; embarrassed ≠ *embarazada*; assist ≠*asistir*; constipated ≠ *constipado*; lecture ≠ *lectura*; library ≠ *librería*

Figure 7.2: False friends in English and Spanish

Multilingual contexts: see page 10

This activity cannot be used with Type A classes. It can be used in Type B classes if there is a language which all the students share, even if the teacher does not speak this language. It is usually very easy to research false friends.

7.4 False friends revision

Outline	Students revise sets of false friends by playing games (bingo, dominoes and Pelmanism).
Level	A1–B2
Time	Approximately 15 minutes
Preparation	No preparation is needed for the bingo activity. For the dominoes, you will need to prepare sets of dominoes (one set for each group of four or five students). These can be done on card or paper. See the example on page 130 (Figure 7.3) for a group of Italian students. For Pelmanism, you will need sets of cards or pieces of paper (one set for each group): on half of these cards write English words or phrases, on the other half, write the equivalents in the students' language. For each false friend that you include in the activity you will need four cards: the English word, its translation, the English word that looks like the translation, and the Italian translation of this word, e.g. *raw*, *crudo* (Italian translation), *crude*, *esplicito* (Italian translation). A pack of between 32 and 48 cards is appropriate.

Procedure (bingo)

1 Tell the students to take a sheet of paper and to divide it into 16 boxes (i.e. 4 x 4). Then tell them to look at their notebooks where they have kept a record of false friends they have previously studied. They should select 16 of these and write them into the boxes. Decide whether you want them to write the English words or the words in their own language.

2 Tell the class that they are going to play bingo. Explain that you will read out translations of the words which they have written in their grid. They should match the words you call out to the words in their grid. When they have a match, they should tick this word. When they have completed a line (horizontal, vertical or diagonal), they should call out 'bingo!'; they have won the game.

3 Call out the false friends that the class has previously studied. Keep a note of the words you have used. When a student calls out 'bingo', ask them to give you the words in their grid and the translations. This acts as a double check for everyone.

Procedure (dominoes)

1 Distribute a set of dominoes to each group. Each domino should contain a word in the students' own language on the left, and an unrelated word in English on the right (i.e. not a matching pair). See examples for Italian students on page 130 (Figure 7.3). The dominoes should be divided equally between the members of the group.

2 Demonstrate the game by drawing one of the dominoes on the board. Ask if anyone can place another domino either side of it: when placed together, two adjacent words must form matching pairs. Students take it in turns to play. If they cannot place a domino, it is the next player's turn. The winner is the first person to get rid of all their dominoes.

3 Students play the game. If appropriate, you could ask them to play a second time.

firma	raw	crudo	be present	assistere	touch	tastare	room
camera	understand	intendere	relative	parente	bald	calvo	camera
macchina fotografica	wait for	attendere	fatal	mortale	crude	esplicito	attend to
curare	parent	genitore	taste	assaggiare	intend to	progettare	fabric
tessuto	compare	confrontare	diary	agenda	confront	affrontare	inevitable
fatale	agenda	ordine del giorno	factory	fabbrica	courageous	baldo	signature

Figure 7.3: False friend dominoes in English and Italian

Procedure (Pelmanism)

1 Distribute a set of cards to each group. These should be spread out and placed face down on a table (or the floor) so that each member of the group can reach them. In the example above, the cards could be cut in half to provide a set of English cards and a set of Italian cards.
2 The object of the game is to find matching pairs of cards. Demonstrate by picking up two cards at random. Look at them, show them to the class, and ask if the cards match. If they do not match, replace the cards face down. It is another player's turn. If they do match, keep the cards and pick up two more cards. This memory game is well known in many cultures around the world and may be familiar to the students.
3 Students play the game, taking it in turns to pick up pairs of cards. If appropriate, you may want them to play a second time.

Multilingual contexts: see page 10
This activity cannot be used with Type A classes. With Type B classes, the bingo version of this revision activity is easier to set up than dominoes or Pelmanism.

7.5 High-frequency English words

Outline	Students explore the use of a high frequency English word.
Level	A2+
Time	Approximately 15 minutes
Preparation	Select a high-frequency English word that it would be useful for your students to study. Lists of high-frequency words are easily found online. The words that work best for this activity are nouns (e.g. *time, people, work, way*), verbs (e.g. *say, know, go, want, work*) and adjectives (e.g. *new, good, first, last*) rather than articles, prepositions and the highest-frequency verbs (e.g. *be, have*).

Use a good dictionary to find six to eight examples of how this word is used in different ways. Simplify the example sentences that are given in the dictionary in order to keep them short and to avoid any other words which the students are unlikely to know.

Translate these sentences into the students' own language. Jumble up the words in the English sentences. Combine these on one worksheet. See the example on page 132 (Figure 7.4) for speakers of German.

Procedure

1 Write the target word on the board. Ask the class if anyone can put the word into a sentence. If there are any suggestions, write two or three of these on the board. If there are no suggestions from the class, provide two or three examples yourself.
2 Organise the class into pairs. The students should translate the examples on the board into their own language. Conduct feedback on this task with the whole class.
3 Distribute the worksheet. Students should do this individually before checking with a partner. Then conduct feedback on the task with the whole class.
4 Students again work with a partner. They should, first, make five or six new sentences using the target word. Then, they should translate these into their own language and write them on a sheet of paper.
5 Students exchange their sheets of paper with other pairs of students, who must translate the sentences back into English.

Multilingual contexts: see page 10

This activity cannot be used if the teacher does not share a language other than English with the students.

Rearrange the words to make translations of the German phrases.

1 Wie macht man das am besten?
  best do the this to **way** what's
  What's the best way to do this?

2 Wir sind weit weg von zuhause.
  a from home long **way** we're

3 Wie geht's nach Hause?
  home is **way** which

4 Wir müssen eine Lösung finden.
  a find must **way** we

5 So mag ich es.
  I it like that's the **way**

6 Ich hab's auf eine andere Weise gemacht.
  another did I it **way**

7 Nur so macht man es.
  do it only that's the to **way**

8 Er hat sich verirrt.
  he his lost **way**

Figure 7.4: Different meanings of *way* in German

7.6 High-frequency English words (collocations)

Outline	Students explore the collocations of a high-frequency English word and its equivalences in their own language.
Level	B1+
Time	Approximately 20 minutes
Preparation	Select a high-frequency English word that it would be useful for your students to study. Lists of high-frequency words are easily found online. The words that work best for this activity are nouns (e.g. *time, people, work, way*), verbs (e.g. *say, know, go, want, work*) and adjectives (e.g. *new, good, first, last*) rather than articles, prepositions and the highest-frequency verbs (e.g. *be, have*).
	Use a good dictionary to help you prepare about ten short example sentences that illustrate how this word is used in different ways. Keep the sentences short and free of any other words which the students are unlikely to know. See the examples (Figure 7.5).

Procedure

1 Dictate the sentences to the class.
2 Tell the students to compare their sentences with a partner. Answer any questions about spelling.
3 Tell the pairs of students to look at the target word in each sentence and to decide how it could be translated into their own language in *two* different ways. Sometimes, of course, the translation of the target word will mean that other words need to be changed, too. This can be done without writing anything down. Give the class three or four minutes to do this before allowing them to use dictionaries.
4 Conduct feedback with the whole class.
5 Tell the pairs of students to look at the list of sentences again and to find one alternative English word (or two, if possible) which could replace the target word in each sentence. Give the class three or four minutes to begin this, before allowing them to use dictionaries. Remind them of the value of cross-checking (see Activity 4.7: *Dictionary cross-checking*).
6 Conduct feedback with the whole class.

great (adjective)	*see* (verb)	*point* (noun)
He's a great guy.	As you see, this is quite difficult.	At some point, you'll need to work harder.
I'm a great film fan.	Can you see me to the airport?	He has a strange point of view.
It was a great opportunity.	I don't see the point of it.	I want to discuss two points.
It was great fun.	I had to see him in his office.	It's only true up to a point.
It's a great big house.	I see what you mean.	She needs two points to win the game.
She's a great friend.	I'll go and see what they want.	The point of the knife is very dangerous.
The great thing about it is the price.	See below for more information.	There's no point talking about it.
They have a great deal of money.	See you later.	What's the point of the meeting?
They're in great danger.	She's not seeing anyone at the moment.	Who invented the decimal point?
We did it in great detail.	They wanted to see my passport.	You've completely missed my point.

Figure 7.5: Collocations with high-frequency words

Multilingual contexts: see page 10

Although this activity is more useful with classes where there is a shared language, it can be used with both Type A and Type B classes.

7.7 Translating concordanced words

Outline	Students study high-frequency words and their collocations/uses.
Level	B1+
Time	15–20 minutes
Preparation	Select a word that you want to focus on. This activity works best with high-frequency words that are used in a variety of ways (e.g. *place, sort, thing, own, mean, just, keep*, etc.). Check the word in a good corpus-driven dictionary (bilingual or monolingual) that your students will have access to. Then, enter the word into a free online concordancer and select eight or nine lines that illustrate the main meanings/uses listed in the dictionary. Cut and paste these lines into something that your students will be able to see (e.g. a handout, a projection, a weblink).

Procedure

1 Show the students the concordanced lines and ask them to translate the highlighted word into their own language. Point out that the word will not always have the same translation for each line. In order to do this, they will need to translate more than just the highlighted word – see the example opposite (Figure 7.6 and Figure 7.7) with *place*. Students should do this work in pairs or small groups. If possible, discourage dictionary use at this stage.
2 Then refer the students to the relevant dictionary entry for this word. Ask them to match the concordanced lines to the dictionary entries.
3 Discuss any difficulties or issues which arise.

Extension

This activity can also work the other way round. Take a similar word in the learners' own language, such as *sitio* in Spanish. First of all, ask the class to brainstorm as many different ways of using this word as they can find. Then, working in pairs or small groups, ask them how the word is translated into English on each occasion. They can refer to dictionaries. With the word *sitio*, for example, the English equivalents would include *spot, room, place, site*, and the use of *sitio* in expressions meaning *somewhere* or *nowhere*. Sorting out high frequency nouns of this kind should be a high priority for any learner.

Note

You can concordance words online with the Compleat Lexical Tutor at www.lextutor.ca or the British National Corpus at www.natcorp.ox.ac.uk.

Multilingual contexts: see page 10

This activity can be used with both Type A and Type B classes.

---

1 In each of the examples, translate the word *place* into your own language.

1 The Test takes PLACE at Cardiff Arms Park on 4 November.

2 The Chelsea Flower Show is probably not the most obvious PLACE to pick up a bargain.

3 In its PLACE, they were erecting a flamboyant, terracotta cathedral

4 Even the unemployed PLACE government policy rather low in a list

5 It was the woman who had put the flowers on the PLACE where Harry Lawrence had died

6 I turned down a PLACE which I had been offered to study theology

7 She had met her connection in the usual PLACE

8 The narrator uses simple nouns in PLACE of more precise terms

9 Lol MacDonald and Kevin Mahoney won with Ron Hill and Dair Rees in second PLACE

Figure 7.6: Exercise using concordanced lines for *place* from the British National Corpus

2 Match the examples 1–9 to the appropriate dictionary entry.

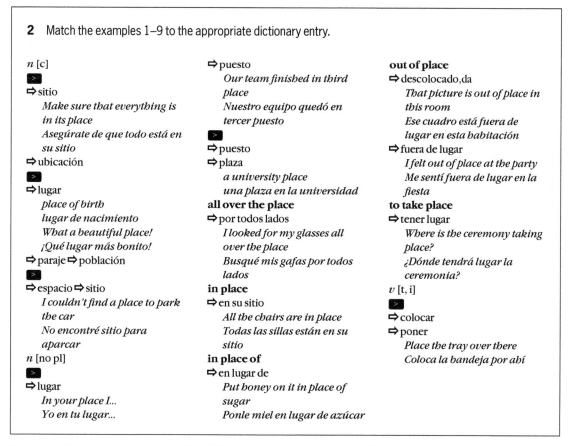

n [c]

⇨ sitio

　Make sure that everything is
　in its place
　Asegúrate de que todo está en
　su sitio

⇨ ubicación

⇨ lugar

　place of birth
　lugar de nacimiento
　What a beautiful place!
　¡Qué lugar más bonito!

⇨ paraje ⇨ población

⇨ espacio ⇨ sitio

　I couldn't find a place to park
　the car
　No encontré sitio para
　aparcar

n [no pl]

⇨ lugar

　In your place I...
　Yo en tu lugar...

⇨ puesto

　Our team finished in third
　place
　Nuestro equipo quedó en
　tercer puesto

⇨ puesto

⇨ plaza

　a university place
　una plaza en la universidad

all over the place

⇨ por todos lados

　I looked for my glasses all
　over the place
　Busqué mis gafas por todos
　lados

in place

⇨ en su sitio

　All the chairs are in place
　Todas las sillas están en su
　sitio

in place of

⇨ en lugar de

　Put honey on it in place of
　sugar
　Ponle miel en lugar de azúcar

out of place

⇨ descolocado,da

　That picture is out of place in
　this room
　Ese cuadro está fuera de
　lugar en esta habitación

⇨ fuera de lugar

　I felt out of place at the party
　Me sentí fuera de lugar en la
　fiesta

to take place

⇨ tener lugar

　Where is the ceremony taking
　place?
　¿Dónde tendrá lugar la
　ceremonia?

v [t, i]

⇨ colocar

⇨ poner

　Place the tray over there
　Coloca la bandeja por ahí

Figure 7.7: Dictionary entry for *place* from Diccionario Cambridge Compact English–Spanish

7.8 Street English

Outline	Students learn and discuss the English that surrounds them in their home environments.
Level	A2–B2
Time	Variable
Preparation	You need a small selection of examples of English that can be found in the shops and streets of your town. Photographs of this language are more interesting than simple transcriptions, but the latter are perfectly adequate. You should be able to find quite easily a range of shop names, brand names, slogans, signs, etc. Some examples have been included on page 137. In addition, a lot of this kind of language can be found on websites (in the students' own language).

Procedure

1 Show a selection of examples of English that you have collected from the shops and streets of your town. Ask the students to work in pairs and translate these into their own language.
2 Draw students' attention to features of the language (e.g. compound nouns) and elicit other examples.
3 Tell the students that, for homework, they must collect further examples of the English that surrounds them in their town. The more they can find, the better.
4 In a subsequent lesson, tell students to share (in small groups) what they have collected. Give them the following tasks.
   • Translate the language into their own language.
   • Discuss and decide why the signs are in English, rather than in their own language (likely reasons include fashion and comprehensibility for tourists).
   • Discuss the reasons why some people are unhappy about the 'invasion of English' and their own feelings about this.

With lower-level students (A2–low B1), the second and third tasks will need to be done in the students' own language.

Note

In many parts of the world, examples of English are all around and can be used as a resource. In more rural locations where 'street English' is comparatively rare, you could focus on well-known English-language international brands (Pizza Hut, Kentucky Fried Chicken, Subway, The Body Shop, Hush Puppies, Caterpillar, Holiday Inn, etc.)

Multilingual contexts: see page 10

This activity cannot be used with Type A classes. It can be used with Type B classes.

7.9 Bilingual word associations

Outline	Students revise a set of vocabulary by associating target words with words in their own language.
Level	A1–B2
Time	Approximately 20 minutes
Preparation	This activity is intended to revise/recycle a set of words that the students have previously studied. Any words can be used except those that are cognates in the students' own language. Select a set of about seven words. Students will need access to bilingual dictionaries in the classroom.

Procedure

1   Dictate the words to the class. In pairs, students (1) compare their spellings and (2) check that they can remember the meanings of these words. Conduct feedback with the whole class and resolve any queries.
2   Tell the students to look at the words on their list again and to write down, next to each word, a word that sounds very similar (or even the same) in their own language. Point out that there are no wrong or right answers, and that they should do this quickly.
3   Tell the students to translate the words they have written in their own language into English. They can use dictionaries for this.
4   Organise the class into pairs. The students should compare their lists of words and find an association between each initial target word and the English words that they obtained by translating the words in their own language that sound like the target words. Give an example or two. Point out that any association, however strange, is acceptable. In the example below (Figure 7.8), one student associated *fit* with *hair* by saying *My cap doesn't fit me when my hair is in a chignon. (chignon* = hair bun)
5   After four or five minutes, elicit some of the ideas that the students have generated. There should be at least a few that are amusing.

Target words	Associations produced by (French-speaking) learners	Meaning of associated word in English
fit (v)	tif	hair
match (v)	match	(sports) match
silk (nU)	cil	eyelash
skirt (nC)	skieur	skier
suit (v)	soutane	soutane
tie (nC)	thaï	Thai
wool (nU)	wallon	Walloon

Figure 7.8: Word associations in English and French

Multilingual contexts: see page 10

This activity can be used with both Type A and Type B classes.

138

7.10 Bilingual drilling

Outline	Students practise grammar or vocabulary through a variety of short oral drills.
Level	A1–B1
Time	No more than five minutes at a time. Keep drills snappy, and use them sparingly.
Preparation	No special preparation required.

Procedure

Bilingual picture drill

If you are teaching a set of vocabulary through large pictures that are visible to the whole class (e.g. drawings or pictures attached to the board, or a wall chart), point to one picture (or one part of a picture) and say the word in English. From time to time, point to a picture and say the wrong English word. If you say the correct word when pointing to a picture, the students must repeat after you. If you say the wrong word when pointing to a picture, the students must call out the translation of the 'wrong' word in their own language.

Accent drill

Many students respond well to drills when they are asked to say the language in a particular way, e.g. happy, sad, scared, very quickly, very slowly, quietly, loudly. A further variation is to ask them to try say the language with an American or British accent. This often works well when you also ask them, from time to time, to say the language in a strong accent of their own language.

Bilingual substitution drill

1 If you want to practise a particular grammar or pronunciation pattern (e.g. sentence stress or intonation), say a model sentence to the class. Everyone must repeat.
2 Then nominate one student to translate this sentence into their own language.
3 Repeat aloud this translation, if it is correct. Then, say it again but change elements of the sentence (e.g. make the verb negative, make the sentence into a question, change pronouns, change a key word).
4 Nominate one student to translate this back into English. If correct, everyone must repeat.
5 Repeat Stages 2–4 as many times as you feel the students are benefitting from the task.

This activity can become a little chaotic if you do not give very explicit instructions. Once students have understood what to do, individual students can also make changes to the previous sentence (see Stage 3).

Multilingual contexts: see page 10

Accent drills can be used with all classes. Bilingual picture drills and bilingual substitution drills cannot be used if the teacher does not share a language, other than English, with the students.

7.11 Word-for-word translation

Outline Students look at a literal translation of a text from English into their own language before attempting to correct a literal translation from their own language into English.

Level All levels

Time Variable (depending on length of text)

Preparation This activity can be used for texts ranging from a few phrases to something much longer. It is most appropriate for focusing attention on particular issues of word order, but can also be used for other areas of grammar (e.g. verb patterns) or vocabulary (especially idioms). Find or write a text in English (Text A) which illustrates the language features that you wish to draw attention to. Translate this word for word into the students' own language (Text B). Find or write a similar text in the students' own language which would normally require the language features you wish to focus on when it is translated into English. Translate this word for word into English (Text C). See example texts opposite (Figure 7.9).

Procedure

1 As an introduction, show the class an English text (Text A) as well as the word-for-word translation in the students' own language (Text B). Ask them to evaluate the translation and to improve it wherever possible.

2 Conduct feedback with the whole class, drawing attention to one or two general points. In the example opposite translating to and from Spanish, the most significant points are probably differences in word order and in set phrases.

3 Show the class a text that has been translated from their language into English, word for word (Text C). Point out that it is as problematic as the text which they just looked at. The students work in pairs to identify and correct the problems.

4 After giving the students a few minutes to work on the text, give them some clues. You could tell them the number of errors that need to be corrected, the type of errors or even the words and phrases that are wrong. Allow the students more time to work in pairs.

5 Conduct feedback with the whole class. You could show them the original Spanish text used to create the word-for-word English translation (Text D).

Text A: English text	Text B: Word-for-word translation into Spanish
A: Hello.	A: Hola.
B: Hello, is Bobby there, please?	B: Hola, ¿Está Bobby, por favor?
A: Speaking.	A: Hablando.
B: Hi, Bobby. It's Salva. Have you got a moment?	B: Hola, Bobby. Está Salva. ¿Tienes un momento?
A: Can you call me back in about five minutes?	A ¿Puedes llamar me de vuelta en más o menos cinco minutos?
B: Sure. No problem.	B: Claro. Ningún problema.

Text C: Word-for-word translation from Spanish	Text D: Spanish text
A: Hello, I am Bobby. Is Salva, please?	A: Hola, soy Bobby. ¿Está Salva, por favor?
B: No, Salva no is in these moments.	B: No, Salva no está en estos momentos.
A: Can you give him a message of my part?	A: ¿Puede darle un recado de mi parte?
A: Yes, obvious.	B: Sí, claro.
B: Can you tell him that him I have called.	A: ¿Puede decirle que le he llamado?
A: Yes, no you worry. Him I will tell that you have called. Bobby, right?	B: Sí, no te preocupes, le diré que has llamado. Bobby, ¿verdad?
A: Yes. Thank you. And forgive the trouble.	A: Sí. Gracias. Y perdone las molestias.

Figure 7.9: Word-for-word translation in English and Spanish

Multilingual contexts: see page 10

This activity cannot be used if the teacher does not share a language other than English with the students.

7.12 Typical mistakes

Outline	Students revise grammar points.
Level	All levels
Time	Variable
Preparation	This activity is intended to revise grammar which the students have previously studied. Prepare a list of common mistakes, spoken or written, that your students continue to make. Select those which are probably caused by interference from their own language. The example below (Figure 7.10) gives typical mistakes made by German students. There are different variations for presenting this list (see *Variations* below), but the simplest is to use a handout or projection where each sentence contains one mistake.

Procedure

1 Tell the students to look at the sentences and to identify the errors, if they can. Give them about three minutes to work on this individually.
2 Allow students to compare their ideas with a partner before conducting feedback with the whole class, and correcting the mistakes.
3 Nominate individual students to translate the correct sentences into their own language. This should be done orally. After each sentence, ask the students to compare the incorrect sentence with the version in their own language. Draw their attention to the parallels between the two.
4 Round off the activity by asking the class if they can think of any other mistakes they sometimes make because their own language 'gets in the way'.

---

1 Had you a good time last night?
2 He speaks very well English.
3 I want that you help me.
4 I will do all what I can.
5 I'd help you, if I would have the time.
6 Let's meet us tomorrow afternoon.
7 One my colleagues lost his job yesterday.
8 The most people go away at the weekend.

Figure 7.10: Typical mistakes made by German students (English level B1-B2)

Variations

To make the work more challenging, you could include a few sentences in the list which are correct. If you do not tell the students how many sentences are correct/incorrect, you will make the exercise a little more challenging still. If you want to make the work less challenging, you could give both the correct and incorrect options and the students' task is to select the appropriate one.

Multilingual contexts: see page 10

This activity cannot be used if the teacher does not share a language, other than English, with the students.

7.13 Homework workshop

Outline	Students collaboratively analyse errors caused by language transfer in their written work (e.g. homework).
Level	A2+
Time	Variable
Preparation	This activity is intended as a follow-up to writing work that the students have done. When marking this work, try to identify errors that have been caused by language transfer. Instead of correcting these (as in the examples below), simply highlight them using a highlighter pen or underline them in a special colour. Other errors may be corrected according to your usual policy. It is useful if students have access to grammar reference books and dictionaries during this lesson.

Procedure

1   Organise the students into small groups of two to four. Hand back the students' written work. Explain that some errors have been highlighted and that this means that you think the mistake was caused because they were translating too directly from their own language. In their groups, the students should look at all the errors of this kind that have been underlined. First, the student whose work it is should translate the English back into their own language. Then, the group should discuss what the problem is, why it arose, and how to correct it. Allow them to refer to grammar reference books and dictionaries.

2   After allowing sufficient time for this group work, bring the whole class together. Ask if there are any unresolved problems, and/or write on the board some examples that you know are causing problems. Elicit suggestions from other students or analyse the problem yourself. Do no more than five or six errors in this way.

3   As a follow-up, suggest that students begin to keep a log of mistakes of this kind. Use this correction policy with subsequent written work that the students do.

In the example on page 143 (Figure 7.11), the highlighted errors are likely to have been caused by over-literal translation: the use of the definite article to make general statements, the doubling of the consonant in *chat*, the use of an infinitive for a modal verb, the use of the preposition *of* after *close*, the use of *do* instead of *make* with *publicity*, the use of the false friend *informations* instead of *news*, and the pluralising of *information*.

15. What do people in general like and dislike about Facebook? (explain)

The people like to chatt with their friends, to can be connected 24/7 and to find some old friends but they dislike facebook because you loose your privacy and because the people broadcast everything.

16. Why do celebrities and ordinary people use Twitter? (explain)

Celebrities:

They want to keep in touch, to be close of the public and the fans. They want to do they own publicity too and to have followers.

Ordinary people:

They want to be connected, to feel alive, to know what's happened in the world, to follow the informations.

Figure 7.11: Student workbook with language transfer errors (French-speaking Belgian student)

Multilingual contexts: see page 10

This activity cannot be used if the teacher does not share a language, other than English, with the students.

7.14 Thème d'imitation

Outline	Students revise language they have previously studied by translating into English a text which is similar to one they have already looked at. Some years ago, this activity was common practice in French classrooms, and is usually referred to by the French expression *Thème d'imitation*.
Level	A2+
Time	Variable
Preparation	Select a text which the students have previously studied. Make a note of the language features of the text which you want the students to practise. In the case of an authentic text, this could be almost anything. In the case of a coursebook text, this could be the discrete language points which the text was written to illustrate. Write a similar or related text in the students' own language which will require the students to use the target language when they translate it into English.

Procedure

1 Distribute copies of the text. Students translate it into English.
2 When they have completed this translation, tell them to look at the text which they had previously studied. Tell them that it contains examples of language which will help them to check or revise the work they have just done. Allow some time for individual work before asking students to compare their ideas with a partner.
3 Conduct feedback with the whole class.
4 If the text is a dialogue (as in the example below), the students can practise it with a partner.

Previously studied text (dialogue)

J: So when are you going?

E: We're leaving on Saturday. We have to get up at 4.30 because we're getting the six o'clock train to the airport.

J: That's early.

E: We don't mind. We're really excited.

J: And where are you staying?

E: We're staying with friends of Ronnie's for the first two weeks – they live in Wellington on North Island. Then we're travelling to the South Island – we're going on a cycling tour for a week.

J: Wow, that sounds like hard work!

Text for translation

A: Donc, vous partez demain?

B: Oui, très tôt. On va prendre un taxi à la gare, parce qu'il faut prendre la navette à cinq heures. On doit être à Charleroi pour faire le check-in deux heures avant notre départ.

A: Dur!

B: Oui, mais au moins on arrive là-bas pas trop tard. On va aller directement de l'aéroport à la plage pour rejoinder les autres.

A: Vous ne voulez pas perdre du temps!

B: Non, on n'y reste que quatre jours.

A: Et vous allez dormir où?

B: On ne sait pas. À la plage, peut-être.

Possible English translation

A: So, you're leaving tomorrow?

B: Yes, really early. We're getting a taxi to the station because we have to get the shuttle-bus at five o'clock in the morning. We have to be in Charleroi for the check-in two hours before the plane leaves.

A: That's tough.

B: Yes, but at least we're arriving there not too late. We're going straight from the airport to the beach to meet up with the others.

A: You don't want to waste any time!

B: No, we're only staying four days.

A: And where are you staying?

B: We don't know. On the beach, perhaps.

Figure 7.12: From Redston, C. & Cunningham, G. (2012) *face2face* Pre-intermediate Second edition, Cambridge: Cambridge University Press, p. 160

Multilingual contexts: see page 10
This activity cannot be used if the teacher does not share a language, other than English, with the students.

Appendix

1 A seminar for teacher training courses (pre-service)

Outline	A seminar for pre-service teachers (e.g. on a Cambridge CELTA or Trinity College London CertTESOL course) which encourages trainees to reflect on using the students' own language in foreign language classes and to become aware of a range of practical options.
Level	Pre-service teachers
Time	Approximately 1 hour
Preparation	You will need to make a sufficient number of photocopies of Handouts A and B, although these could also be projected onto the board. In addition, you will need photocopies of a range of practical activities (one each) from either this book or another source. You will need approximately one different activity for each trainee. Select a variety of different activity types, making sure that you include a good number of basic techniques (see Chapter 2).

Note

You could use Activity 3, *Classroom observation task*, in conjunction with this task.

Procedure

1 Put trainees into small groups. Ask them to discuss their own language learning experiences. Write the following questions on the board to guide the discussion.
   - How much did your teachers use your language in class? For what purposes?
   - How often did you, as a learner, translate from and into the target language?
   - Do you think you might have learned more quickly if your teacher had used more or less of your own language?

2 Draw trainees' attention to the advertisement in Handout A. Highlight the phrase *Only English spoken in class*. Ask the trainees why they think the school has decided to focus on this in their advertisement. Put trainees into groups and ask them to brainstorm as many reasons as possible for why an English-only policy might be considered to be a good thing.

Handout A

✓ Small groups

✓ Native-speaker teachers

✓ Only English spoken in class

✓ Guaranteed results

Schaerbeek - School of English

From *Translation and Own-language Activities* © Cambridge University Press 2014   PHOTOCOPIABLE

3 When trainees have had enough time to brainstorm their ideas (five minutes is probably sufficient), elicit their ideas and make a list on the board. You may also wish to add to the list yourself. Do not, at this stage, get into a discussion about the rights and wrongs of these reasons.

4 Distribute Handout B. Ask trainees to compare the notes on the board with the points on the handout. Ask them to identify any points that were not listed on the board. A few minutes should be sufficient for this. Conduct feedback with the whole group.

Handout B

A The most powerful reason for an English-only policy in a language school is commercial. It seems that most people (i.e. customers) believe that a native-speaker teacher who uses only English makes the best teacher. Of course, it is possible that the native-speaker teacher is unable to speak the language of the students and is, therefore, necessarily restricted to English only.

B Apart from the point above, the most commonly quoted reason for adopting an English-only policy is that any time spent speaking the students' own language is time that could have been spent speaking English. English-only therefore equals maximum opportunities for speaking English.

C It is often said that language learners need to learn to think in the target language. Permitting the use of the student's own language discourages them from, and makes it harder to start, doing so.

D It is said that using the students' own language results in greater first language interference than when an English-only policy is adopted.

E It is said that translation encourages learners to assume falsely that there are equivalences between the two languages. This can lead, for example, to problems with false friends.

F Using the students' own language is sometimes seen as 'unnatural'. Infants learning their first language do not refer to other languages. If we equate first language learning with the learning of other languages, it follows that only one language should be used.

G It is said that translation is not a useful real-life skill, so there is no point in practising it in the classroom (except for people who are training to be translators).

From *Translation and Own-language Activities* © Cambridge University Press 2014   PHOTOCOPIABLE

---

5 Ask the group to consider the reasons that have been listed on the board. Ask if anyone would take issue with any of them. Then distribute copies of Handout C. Ask trainees to match the quotations on Handout C to the points that are listed on Handout B. This can be done individually and then checked in pairs.

Handout C

1 Grammatical phenomena which are subject to interference from L1 might lend themselves well to translation exercises in order to prevent the development of undesirable language habits.

2 Many scholars now agree that 'the language of thought for all but the most advanced L2 learners is inevitably his/her L1'.

3 Translation is one of the most authentic activities imaginable as it is done constantly in 'real' life – outside the classroom – and in many cases is the only activity connected with the foreign language that our students will be involved in later on.

4 Translation is intrinsically inherent in foreign language learning since the foreign learner normally has already acquired a comprehensive lexical, conceptual, grammatical, communicative and phonetic competence in his or her L1 when beginning to learn the other language. Thus, implicitly s/he is, at least in the initial and intermediate stages of foreign language learning, procedurally referring to these deeply ingrained categories, norms and patterns when being confronted with items in the other language.

5 Word-for-word translation is something that takes place anyway – whether we want it to happen or not, whether we consider it useless or not. At least when words with lexical meanings are concerned, we can be sure that they automatically activate their L1-partners in the mental lexicon. If this process takes place anyway, it would obviously be best to make use of it instead of trying to quell it.

6 Even in a classroom setting which uses a predominantly intralingual strategy, it is advisable to allow certain well-defined periods in which the use of the L1 is allowed so that questions can be asked, meanings can be verified, uncertainties can be removed, and explanations given which would not be accessible to the learner in L2.

7 Translation has been too long in exile, for all kinds of reasons which … have little to do with any considered pedagogic principle. It is time it was given a fair and informed appraisal.

References

1 Stern, H.H. & Allen, P. & Harley, B. (eds.) (1992) *Issues and Options in Language Teaching*, Oxford: Oxford University Press, p. 294.
2 Turnbull, M. & Dailey-O'Cain, J. (eds.) (2009) *First Language Use in Second and Foreign Language Learning*, Bristol: Multilingual Matters, p. 5, citing Macaro (2005) 'Codeswitching in the L2 Classroom: A communication and learning strategy'. In Llurda (ed.) *Non-Native Language Teachers: Perceptions, Challenges and Contributions to the Profession*, New York: Springer, pp. 63–84.
3 Grellet, F. (1991) *Apprendre à Traduire*, Nancy: Presses Universitaires de Nancy, p. 11.
4 Witte, A., Harden, T. & Ramos de Oliveira Harden, A. (2009) 'Translation and Second Language Learning: General Considerations' in Witte, A., Harden, T. & Ramos de Oliveira Harden, A. (eds.) (2009) *Translation in Second Language Learning and Teaching*, Bern: Peter Lang, p .4.
5 Hentschel, E. (2009) 'Translation as an inevitable part of Foreign Language Acquisition' in Witte, A., Harden, T. & Ramos de Oliveira Harden, A. (eds.) (2009) *Translation in Second Language Learning and Teaching*, Bern: Peter Lang, p. 23.
6 Stern, H.H. & Allen, P. & Harley, B. (eds.) (1992) *Issues and Options in Language Teaching*, Oxford: Oxford University Press, p. 298.
7 Widdowson, H. (2003) *Defining Issues in English Language Teaching*, Oxford: Oxford University Press, p. 160.

6   Conduct feedback with the whole group.

Feedback notes

Answer key: 1D, 2C, 3G, 4F, 5E, 6B, 7A

You could summarise the current consensus among researchers as: it is not a question of whether or not teachers should use the students' own language in the English language classroom, but a question of how and how often. Guy Cook writes that there is 'an array of recent evidence and argument in favour of reincorporating students' own languages into language teaching, and a corresponding disquiet that they were ever excluded' (Cook, 2010, p. 51), and continues 'in short, there is a considerable current of opinion in favour of a return to cross-lingual teaching' (p. 52).

7   Display the photocopied activities and techniques on walls or desks around the room. Tell trainees to stand up and move around the room reading as many of these practical ideas as possible. Set a time limit of ten minutes.
8   Organise trainees into groups of four or five. Tell them to share the practical ideas they have discovered and to answer the following questions:
    1   Which activities did you like most and least?
    2   What problems might you have with these activities in a classroom?
9   Close the session with a whole-group opportunity for further discussion and questions.

References

Cook, G. (2010) *Translation in Language Teaching*, Oxford: Oxford University Press.

2 A seminar for teacher development courses (in-service)

Outline	A seminar for in-service teachers which encourages them to reflect on using the students' own language in foreign language classes and to extend their range of practical options.
Level	In-service teachers
Time	Approximately 1 hour
Preparation	You will need to make a sufficient number of photocopies of Handout A, although this could also be projected onto the board. In addition, you will need photocopies of a range of practical activities (one each) from either this book or another source. You will need approximately one different activity for each trainee. Select a variety of different activity types, making sure that you include a good number of basic techniques (see Chapter 2).

Note

You could use Activity 3, *Classroom observation task*, in conjunction with this task.

Procedure

1 Put participants into groups. Write the questions below on the board and ask participants to discuss them. Allow approximately ten minutes.
   - How often, and for what reasons, do you use the students' own language in the classroom?
   - Do you think your approach is similar or different to the majority of your colleagues?
   - In terms of using the students' own language, how similar or different is your approach to the teachers who taught you English?

   Conduct feedback with the whole group. You will probably need about another ten minutes for this.

Feedback notes

Research indicates that the amount of time that teachers spend using the students' own language varies enormously (from zero to as much as 90%!), although a probable average is about 20% (Levine, 2012).

Research also suggests that many teachers significantly underestimate the amount of time they spend using their students' own language (Copland & Neokleous, 2011, p. 271). This is probably because they feel guilty about using the students' language.

The reasons for using the students' own language include: explaining language, administrative matters, managing interpersonal relations (including discipline and humour) There is enormous variation in the amount of time that teachers spend using the students' language for these different functions.

---

2 Distribute the handout. Ask participants to read the text and then discuss their response with a partner.

Should we have a policy of English-only in the classroom?

It is said that …	but …
you learn English by using it, so any time that is spent using your own language is time that could have been spent practising English …	… some use of the students' own language (especially at lower levels) may save time, improve understanding and reassure the learners. It may even result in greater amounts of English being spoken.
learners need to learn to think in English (and not in their own language) and it is much harder to do this if they are allowed to speak their own language …	… research suggests that the 'language of thought' for everyone, except for those with a very high level, is one's own language. Most of our students do not need, and will not achieve, such a high level, so it is counterproductive to insist on something that they cannot do and it is pointless to encourage them to aspire to something which is unrealistic.
learners need to learn English through English so that they do not make mistakes that are caused by first language interference (such as false friends) …	… research suggests that the direct contrast of English with the students' own language may be the best way to clarify problems of language transfer.
languages are best learned in a natural way, in the same way that children learn their first language, without other languages getting in the way …	… all learning is built upon what we already know, and learners will inevitably make comparisons between English and other languages they know, whether we like it or not. What's more, first language acquisition is very different from the acquisition of other languages: there are no good reasons for equating one with the other.
most students do not need to become translators …	… translation is one of the most natural and frequent activities in real-life situations where two languages are involved.
a very powerful reason for an English-only policy is commercial. Many people believe that a native-speaker teacher who uses only English makes the best teacher …	… there is no evidence that a policy of English-only produces better results. There is, however, evidence that (all other things being equal) students will benefit from having a teacher who speaks their own language and understands their problems.

If you are interested in following up the theoretical and research arguments …

Cook, G. (2010) *Translation in Language Teaching*, Oxford: Oxford University Press.
Hall, G. & Cook, G. (2012) 'Own language use in language teaching and learning.' *Language Teaching*, 45, pp. 271–308.
    Available online at: http://journals.cambridge.org. [Last accessed 23 August 2013]

3   Ask the group the following question: why do you think that many teachers and institutions believe that English-only is the best policy, despite the fact that the research suggests the opposite?

4   Display the photocopied activities and techniques on walls or desks around the room. Tell trainees to stand up and move around the room reading as many of these practical ideas as possible. Set a time limit of ten minutes.

5   Organise trainees into groups of four or five. Tell them to share the practical ideas they have discovered and to answer the following questions:

   1   Which activities did you like most and least?

   2   What problems might you have with these activities in a classroom?

6   Close the session with a whole-group opportunity for further discussion and questions.

References

Cook, G. (2010) *Translation in Language Teaching*, Oxford: Oxford University Press.

Copland, F. & Neokleous, G. (2011) 'L1 to teach L2: complexities and contradictions' *ELT Journal* Vol 65/3, pp. 270–80. Available online by subscription at: http://eltj.oxfordjournals.org. [Last accessed 23 August 2013]

Hall, G. & Cook, G. (2012) 'Own language use in language teaching and learning.' *Language Teaching*, 45, pp 271–308. Available online at: http://journals.cambridge.org. [Last accessed 23 August 2013]

Levine, G.S. (2012) 'Principles for code choice in the foreign language classroom: A focus on grammaring.' *Language Teaching*, available on CJO2012. Available online at: http://journals.cambridge.org. [Last accessed 23 August 2013]

3 Classroom observation task

Outline	Teachers or trainee teachers observe a lesson and reflect on the use of different languages in the classroom.
Level	Suitable for both pre-service and in-service teachers
Time	30 minutes approximately (in addition to observation time)
Preparation	Photocopy one observation task sheet for each participant. Use Observation task A if the lesson to be observed is one where the majority of students speak the same language as the teacher (e.g. in a high school or university setting). This task focuses primarily on the teacher. Use Observation task B if the lesson to be observed is one where there is a wide variety of first languages in the classroom and where all (or almost all) language talk is in English (e.g. in a language school in an English-speaking country). This task focuses primarily on the students.

Procedure

The way that you manage this activity will depend to a large extent on the possibilities that are open to you to arrange observation of classes. If possible, arrange for participants to observe lower-level (B1 or below) classes. The most likely scenarios are (1) more than one observer observing the same lesson, (2) observers observe different lessons. Live observation is usually much more interesting than recorded classes on video, but the latter have the advantage of allowing everyone in the group to refer to the same lesson.

1 Distribute the relevant observation task and check that everyone understands what is required. If necessary, remind participants of the etiquette of observing other teachers' classes.
2 After the observations, participants work in pairs or small groups and compare their notes to Parts 1, 2 and 3 of the observation tasks.
3 Bring the whole group together for discussion of part 4 of the task.

Notes

1 This activity can be used on teacher training or teacher development programmes in conjunction with Activities 1, *A seminar for teacher training courses (pre-service)*, and 2, *A seminar for teacher development courses (in-service)*.
2 The observation tasks can also be used to reflect on one's own teaching.

Observation task A

Before the class begins, quickly read through all the questions. Make notes on these questions during the lesson.

Part 1

1   Do all the students in the class speak the same language?

   If there are speakers of other languages, how well do they speak the majority language of the classroom?

   If there are speakers of other languages, are they mixed up with the rest of the class or do they sit together?

   Did the segregation or integration of minority language students have any impact on what took place in the lesson?

2   How well can the teacher speak the languages of the students?

Part 2

1   Note down any occasions when the teacher speaks the majority language of the class. Try to identify the reasons.

   Note down any occasions when the teacher used one of the minority languages of the class. Try to identify the reasons.

2   If possible, have a look at some of the students' notes/notebooks at the end of the lesson. Have they used their own language in their notes? If so, for what reasons?

Part 3

1   Estimate the proportion of teacher talk that was in a language other than English.

2   When would it have been possible for the teacher to use English rather than the students' language? How would English have affected (a) the clarity or comprehensibility of what the teacher wanted to say, (b) the students' response to what the teacher was saying, (c) the flow of the lesson?

3   How would the lesson have been different if the teacher had used only English?

Part 4

Do you think any of these students would prefer to be, or benefit from being, in a multilingual group where English is the only language that is used?

Observation task B

Before the class begins, quickly read through all the questions. Make notes on these questions during the lesson.

Part 1

1 Do all the students in the class speak the same language?

 If not, how many different languages do they speak?

2 Are any students using a lingua franca other than English to communicate among themselves?

3 How well can the teacher speak the languages of the students?

Part 2

1 Does the seating arrangement of the class have any connection with the students' languages? For example, are students with a shared language (this might be their first, second or even third language) sitting together?

 In this class, who decided who sits where: the teacher or the students themselves?

2 Did the seating arrangement (in relation to the students' shared languages) have any impact on what took place in the lesson? For example, did this facilitate or prevent communication between students in their own languages?

3 Should teachers take the students' own languages into account when deciding who sits where?

Part 3

1 Note down any occasions when students speak their own language. Try to identify the reasons.

2 If possible, have a look at some of the students' notes/notebooks at the end of the lesson. Have they used their own language in their notes? If so, for what reasons?

Part 4

Do you think any of these students would prefer to be, or benefit from being, in a monolingual group with a teacher who can speak their own language?

Index